TO
LISTEN
TO A CHILD

Books by T. Berry Brazelton, M.D.

ON BECOMING A FAMILY
The Growth of Attachment Before and After Birth

INFANTS AND MOTHERS
Differences in Development

TODDLERS AND PARENTS
Declaration of Independence

DOCTOR AND CHILD

TO LISTEN TO A CHILD
Understanding the Normal Problems of Growing Up

WORKING AND CARING

WHAT EVERY BABY KNOWS

FAMILIES, CRISIS, AND CARING

TOUCHPOINTS
Your Child's Emotional and Behavioral Development

with Bertrand G. Cramer, M.D.

THE EARLIEST RELATIONSHIP
Parents, Infants and the Drama of Early Attachment

TO LISTEN TO A CHILD

UNDERSTANDING THE NORMAL PROBLEMS OF GROWING UP

T. BERRY BRAZELTON, M.D.

Photographs by B.A. King

A Merloyd Lawrence Book

ADDISON-WESLEY PUBLISHING COMPANY
Reading, Massachusetts   Menlo Park, California   New York
Don Mills, Ontario   Wokingham, England   Amsterdam   Bonn
Sidney   Singapore   Tokyo   Madrid   San Juan   Paris
Seoul   Milan   Mexico City   Taipei

Copyright © 1984 by T. Berry Brazelton, M.D.

Parts of the material in Chapters 2 through 10 and 12 through 14 first appeared, in different form, in *Redbook* Magazine.

Portions of Chapter 1 are excerpted from the book *Child Health Encyclopedia: The Complete Guide for Parents* by the Children's Hospital Medical Center and Richard I. Feinbloom, M.D. © 1975 by the Children's Hospital Medical Center and Richard I. Feinbloom, M.D. Reprinted by permission of Delacorte Press/Seymour Lawrence. A Merloyd Lawrence Book.

Library of Congress Cataloging in Publication Data

Brazelton, T. Berry, 1918–
  To listen to a child.

  "A Merloyd Lawrence book."
  Includes index.
  1. Children—Care and hygiene. 2. Children—Mental
health. 3. Problem children. 4. Parent and child.
5. Child development. I. Title.
RJ61.B83 1984   155.4   84-6174
ISBN 0-201-10554-3 (paperback)
ISBN 0-201-63270-5 (paperback)

Cover design by Marshall Henrichs
Cover photograph by Barbara Campbell, reprinted by permission of *Redbook* Magazine. © 1982 by The Hearst Corporation. All rights reserved.

Text design by Dana Kasarsky Design, New York, NY
Set in 11 point ITC Garamond by Waldman Graphics, Inc., Pennsauken, NJ

Printed in the United States of America

1 2 3 4 5 6 7 8 9-DO-9695949392
First printing, September 1992

CONTENTS

1 / INTRODUCTION   **1**

PART ONE
LOVE AND FEARS

2 / HOW BABIES LEARN ABOUT LOVE   **21**
3 / FEARS IN SMALL CHILDREN   **33**
4 / WHEN A CHILD IS SAD   **45**
5 / THUMBSUCKING AND LOVEYS: STEPS
TOWARDS INDEPENDENCE   **55**
6 / SPACING CHILDREN   **69**

PART TWO
COMMON ISSUES

7 / DISCIPLINE   **81**
8 / FEEDING: PLEASURE OR BATTLEGROUND?   **93**
9 / SLEEP   **107**

PART THREE
PSYCHOSOMATIC PROBLEMS

10 / STOMACHACHES AND HEADACHES   **125**

11 / HANDLING CROUP, SEIZURES AND OTHER
ACUTE EMERGENCIES   **137**

12 / ASTHMA   **145**

13 / BEDWETTING: WHOSE SUCCESS IS IT?   **157**

14 / LISTENING TO THE HOSPITALIZED CHILD   **167**

ABOUT THE AUTHOR   **178**

INDEX   **179**

ACKNOWLEDGMENTS

For Chris
who has pressed me to learn to listen

The author would like to thank the editors of Redbook *Magazine, who have fostered his thinking about the ideas in this book. Sey Chassler, Amy Levin, Kitty Ball Ross, Jean Evans, Annette Capone, and Sara Nelson have all been of immense support.*

1
INTRODUCTION

Transient periods of "problem" behavior are an inevitable part of any child's normal development. For instance, nearly all children go through a period of stuttering while learning to speak. As they are trying to identify with their parents, the struggle produces other predictable problems. Children often steal from their parents in the fourth and fifth years, by way of trying to capture a part of them. They lie to them by way of testing them. Although these are transient symptoms, they can be frightening ones. Stomachaches in little girls and bedwetting in little boys are more expectable than they are unusual (see Chapters 10 and 13). These deviations from the straight path toward a healthy, reasonably problem-free adulthood fulfill a purpose. It seems most children must explore or experience them while learning the limits of acceptable behavior.

Most of these "normal problems" turn out to be time-limited, associated with certain stages in the child's development. During this period the child must meet the standards of a demanding environment. Our family life in the United States creates high expectations; an emotionally healthy child has an enormous desire to live up to them. Of course, he or she* will need a time for pulling back, for

---

*To avoid the exclusive use of male pronouns, I will use "he" for the child in one chapter and "she" for the next.

looking over the situation, for recharging. I see this as an economical way of managing constant demands. A temporary period of deviation into rebellious, unacceptable behavior strengthens the periods of successful conformity. Thus, for the child, this deviant behavior and these periods of testing are necessary and important.

For the parent, however, they may be very stressful. They may call up unresolved issues in the parents' own past—the memory of a brother who was a bedwetter until he was twelve, or a sister whose appendix ruptured when no one took her bellyache seriously. Also, "problem" behavior may well be seen by parents as a symptom of failure on their part. Unless parents can see these symptoms as transient, as serving a healthy purpose, they are likely to try vigorously to eradicate them. Parents fear that to ignore them would be a sign of not caring or of being a lazy parent, or that if they wait too long, the child might get set in "bad habits," either to get attention or to fall back on them as a crutch. For these reasons parents try to stop a child from thumbsucking or from masturbation, for instance. Parents also tend to reinforce a child's anxiety about a complaint such as a stomachache. We now know that either of these reactions is likely to set, rather than interrupt, the pattern. Instead, understanding of the process and a detached, supportive approach is more likely to allow the child to work out his own pattern of progress. But how many caring parents would come to that realization easily?

This book is an attempt to bring some of these common issues into the open. I would like to lay out for parents the developmental reasons for fears, thumbsucking, eating and sleeping problems, and psychosomatic complaints, and to suggest ways of looking at and dealing with them. I hope to help parents see their roles more objectively, and to make choices about their own behavior which would avoid setting up tension or deepening the guilt that a child may feel about this "deviant" behavior when it develops. Tension and guilt are likely to compound the problem, setting it into more permanent patterns. An understanding of the child's developmental needs can help a parent relax and allow the child's own drive toward health take over.

First of all, it is important for parents to realize that their ability to shape a child's behavior is limited by individual differences, present at birth. At birth, we see infants who overreact to every noise or stimulus—starting visibly, crying out, changing color, spitting up, and having a bowel movement—all as part of a reaction to a single stimulus. Other infants will react to the same stimulus by lying quietly in their cribs, eyes widening, faces alerting, color paling, and bodily activity reducing to a minimun, seeming to conserve all energy in order to pay attention to the stimulus. These are both normal reactions, at different ends of a spectrum. The involvement of the infant's whole body is apparent; attention and psychological mechanisms are intimately tied to physiological reactions. As babies get older, their physiological reactions may appear less connected to their personalities. This lack of connection is more apparent than real, for there are well-defined psychophysiological (mind-body) differences in reactivity among individuals of all ages. A challenging environment will reinforce certain physiological patterns as the infant tries to handle the stress. The mechanisms that one infant uses will differ markedly from those that another may use. For instance, one infant may resort to crying—insistently and for long periods—as a way of shutting out the tension of an overwrought mother. Another may begin to withdraw into more and more sleep. Both reactions are ways of coping with stress that might otherwise overload the baby's system, and they may become the pattern on which a particular child falls back whenever under stress. As children grow, they may outgrow this pattern or it may survive in the kind of bodily reaction each demonstrates as a response to pressure from the outside—the first kind of person reacting with anger, flushing, and other symptoms of violent reaction that all remain on the surface, whereas the second person may become quieter, more withdrawn and pale, suffering internally but showing little of it to the outside world. Although the second type may be an easier one for others to live with, the first person may suffer less in the long run.

While parents cannot change these individual differences, they have some control over their own reactions to their child's behavior. Often an eager or anxious parent will focus attention on and over-emphasize a routine event, such as thumbsucking, which is in itself of no importance, and reinforce it until it is a problem. All babies suck their thumbs, and will give up sucking in time as their interest in other pleasures increases (see Chapter 5). But parents who are concerned with this sucking may try to stop it. In their efforts to stop the thumbsucking, they increase the baby's frustration. They create tension for the infant whose only way of relieving tension may be to suck his thumb. So the parents' efforts end up reinforcing the very symptom they are trying to relieve, and the child begins to use the physical act to elicit a predictable parental response, to express a feeling, or to let off tension.

As another example, spitting up milk after feedings is common in infants. Since it is objectionable to parents, it is hard for them to see that it could become pleasurable for an infant. However, it can become a way of handling tension, frustration, and even appears to be satisfying for certain infants whose environments are not providing other, more satisfying experiences. Spitting up milk and chewing on it is called rumination. Rumination is a rare but dramatic symptom which turns up in the last half of the first year in certain infants. As they lie in bed between meals, they make themselves regurgitate their food, chew on it as a cow does on her cud, and then swallow the milk curds, again and again. This behavior has been associated with social deprivation in children and was first recognized in babies who were not getting enough stimulation from their environments.

Another group of ruminators are not deprived of stimulation from their environment but suffer from inappropriate stimulation. The kind of stimulation they receive is unacceptable to them as individuals. An infant at Children's Hospital ruminated whenever we overstimulated her—whenever there was too much noise or confusion, or after a tense, hurried nurse had fed her. As she began to spit up, those caring for her rushed to distract her, to occupy her attention so that she wouldn't lose her meal. Although these efforts staved off her symptom for the moment, she waited until she was alone, then proceeded to disgorge her entire meal—as if she'd waited to discharge all of the extra internal stress caused by the excess attention.

As we reconstructed the evolution of this symptom with her mother, we found that she had begun to spit up as a new baby, just as many infants do, but her spitting continued throughout her first nine months of life. The family was under a great deal of stress at the time, and this baby's normal spitting up became upsetting to the mother. She overreacted to it, feeling that the baby was abnormal and might die unless she corrected this tendency to spit up. With her physician's help, she tried to rule out every possible cause, frantically changing formulas, holding her propped up after feedings, having her intestinal tract X-rayed, and so forth. After each new episode of spitting, she overreacted, and soon the baby was set in a pattern of spitting up more and more. At first, this may have been the result of overstimulation. As it became a regular pattern, it also became the baby's reaction to any stress around her. As we became able to understand the evolution of this symptom pattern, we reduced the stimulation and the anxiety around each feeding, substituting an affectionate nurse to sit quietly and sing to her. The baby responded within a week! She not only stopped ruminating after feedings, but began to gain weight. We shared our insight with the mother, helped her with her own anxiety about the infant, and reunited them in unstressed feeding situations under supervision in the hospital. Now that this symptom no longer alarms the mother, she and her baby are thriving with each other. (For discussion of feeding problems and emotional factors, see Chapter 8).

Parents are likely to focus on a common developmental aberration and reinforce it as a pattern at any age. They are likely to do so for unconscious reasons and may not be aware of their role in reinforcing the behavior until it is already a habit. Even at this point it is not too late to relieve tension for the child, and to break the vicious circle. The experience of alleviating a disturbing symptom can then become a learning experience from which both child and parents can gather strength.

Each age has its natural stresses and it would be beyond the scope of this book to discuss each one. But, there are certain age-related physical or psychological symptoms that crop up regularly. By recognizing them as normal, transitory signs of development, parents can avoid setting them up as problem areas.

First Year

Colic and crying—normally two–three hours per day in the first three months

Spitting up after feedings

Thumb- or fingersucking

Infrequent bowel movements in a breast-fed baby

Constipation—hard bowel movements which can be softened by changes in diet

Waking at night just prior to developmental spurts

Feeding refusals associated with wanting to feed self at 8 months or so

Second Year

Feeding aberrations—refusing one food after another, eating only one meal a day

Temper tantrums and breath holding spells

Withholding stools and problems around toilet training—usually from training instituted too early and too much pressure to conform

Fourth to Sixth Year

Headaches or sick stomachs in boys just before school

Bellyaches in girls

Tics, masturbation, lying, stealing, fears, and nightmares, especially in boys as they develop aggressive feelings they can't handle during the day

Transient periods of bedwetting (enuresis) in boys

Early School Years

Overreaction to illness, to injury
Using illness to substitute for school fears
Constipation
Occasional bedwetting during illness or hospitalization
Headaches due to tension
Stomachaches due to tension

Adolescence

Lack of appetite or anorexia
Overeating
Delayed onset of menstruation
Concern about body image, associated with early or delayed
    development

Many of the symptoms named above are surprisingly common as children develop. They often become of concern to the child himself. If parents add their own overreaction, they are redoubling anxiety in the child. Children are able to handle their own concern, but not that of their parents'. If parents block communication by, for example, being overly strict or punitive, the child may settle on the physical complaint as a safe way of getting attention or otherwise dealing with the adult.

When the child expresses concern about a symptom, there is a fine line between the possibility of the parents' overlooking a possibly serious disorder or neglecting the child's genuine needs or, on the other hand, taking it too seriously and emphasizing its value in his mind. When a child has a pain, parents must first make sure it isn't serious. They then can reassure the child, both by their attitude and by their having checked it out, that he needn't be overconcerned either. If it is ignored, the child may have to try harder to get the parents' attention (see Chapter 10 on stomachaches, headaches).

In older children, when symptoms are occurring frequently and are obvious bids for parental attention, they should become a red flag, indicating that there are other underlying problems. If the child needs a symptom to express his conflicts, he needs a parent's solid attention to his worries. For instance, take a headache which is caused by the tension of facing school. If the parents allow the child to lie down or stay home from school, they add reinforcement to the problem. Since the real problem is that of dealing with the anxiety about leaving home and handling the adjustment to schoolwork, teachers, and peers, a parent who wants to help must look beyond the headache. If parents dodge their opportunity to examine the underlying anxiety about separating, about facing responsibility, they contribute to the childs' problem in growing up, and they may be tightening the attachment bonds which are difficult enough for the child to loosen. Instead, if parents can talk to the child about the reasons for this anxiety over separation and school, the headaches often decrease. Just offering an aspirin and not talking directly is as bad as ignoring a symptom in the hope that it will go away. Physicians, too, dodge their responsibility to help parents and children by such advice as, "He'll grow out of it." Parents usually can look behind the symptom to reasons for anxiety, and then interpret them to the child. This not only will bring the underlying worries to a level of consciousness where both can deal with them, but it also will demonstrate to the child that his parents care, understand, and want to help.

Although direct questioning is not likely to uncover the real reasons for a child's anxiety or distress, when a parent hits upon the right area while talking, it is obvious. Children let you know by a facial sign or a visible change in attitude when a sore spot is touched upon. They may relax and smile, or they may turn away or change the subject. Fear of going to school makes a good example. If it is not expressed directly in words, it may surface as a physical complaint like belly pain in the morning. Commonly, it is a combination of anxiety about growing up, coupled with fears about what might happen while the child is away at school. A mother or father can approach these feelings and encourage a child to talk by saying such things as, "I think you are worried about going to school. Maybe you are upset by your teacher, and maybe by the other children. But I really think you just hate to leave home and me. It is hard to grow up, but you are getting bigger and I must help you become a big, independent boy;" or, "Maybe you are worried about what will happen to me while you are gone. Nothing will happen. It is really up to me to take care of myself—not up to you. Perhaps the reason you worry about me is that you sometimes wish something would happen to me. All children get angry with their parents and wish that something bad would happen. But wishing at times like that won't make it come true, and you don't need to be afraid of your wishes. Maybe this is why you won't go to school sometimes." If the child listens, but changes the subject afterward, the mother can suspect that she has hit the nail on the head. Such an interpretation may help the child understand himself. The two techniques, attentive listening and helping him to understand his reasons for a symptom, are effective in many, many instances—especially in normally developing children. They are extensions of good, open communication between parent and child, and are important as such (see Chapter 2 on fears).

In addition to recognizing fears and tension behind complaints without physiological causes, parents also should be aware that any illness can be reinforced by anxiety. Croup (see Chapter 11) is a good example. It is an acute difficulty in breathing and is a common complication of colds in small children. It always comes on suddenly, usually in the middle of the night. The child is acutely hoarse and breathes in with a loud, croaking noise. As a result of this trouble in breathing, he becomes frightened. Since the difficulty is located in the larynx (or voice box) and is due to a swelling of the tissues which then interfere with the size of his airway, there is less air coming into his lungs. As he panics, his need for oxygen increases and he begins to breathe more shallowly and rapidly. The tension brings about a spasm of the larynx, which acts to cut down the size of the airway further. Steam is a specific antidote which both relaxes the spasm and reduces the tissue swelling, thereby quickly facilitating the passage of air through the partially obstructed airway. If parents can respond to the child's anxiety with reassurance, calming and comforting him, and sitting with him in a room cloudy with steam, 95% of croup complaints can be alleviated quickly and at home. If, on the other hand, their anxiety adds to the child's own, the spasm of his larynx will increase with his fear, and emergency hospitalization may become necessary. Unfortunately, hospital experience may frighten him further, and as a last resort, surgery may become necessary to relieve the obstructed airway. So, the parents' first job is to protect their child from serious complications by dealing with their own anxiety, rather than transmitting it to the child.

"Inherited" psychosomatic disorders are even more likely to arouse anxiety in parents. When parents have had a problem with a particular disease or symptom, it is very likely that they will reinforce it if it occurs in one of their children. For example, a child with his first attack of asthma is likely to be frightened by his inability to breathe properly. If a father who has allergies, has had asthma, and knows how frightening it is, becomes excited, overreacts, and transmits his own anxiety, the child's problems are magnified. The physical component of an allergy is inheritable, and we are not in any way denying this inherited tendency. But the organic (physical) disorder may be quickly aggravated by overattention. In some cases, anxiety interferes with a parent's capacity to use simple, effective remedies. We have seen many allergic parents who, in denying their anxiety about asthma, can't hear us when we suggest that ridding a house of a cat or of feather pillows might help cut down the allergens in the household for the child. They wait too long before they give medication to break up a frightening cycle for the child. They wait because they keep hoping the wheezing will disappear. As a child's tension builds up, it is expressed in more labored breathing, and there becomes less and less likelihood of his being able to break the cycle easily. Over a period of time, such a disease becomes a way of expressing all anxiety. We see a 3- or 4-year-old child wheezing actively as he watches his mother's anxious face. When the parent leaves the room, and a more objective nurse or physician takes over, the child's anxiety and wheezing subside. This is not a magical form of medicine, nor even a difficult one to understand. (For a discussion of asthma, see Chapter 12.)

In summary, symptoms such as those mentioned above are not "faked" by the child; nor does it help to think of them as weakness on the child's part. Trying to shame or punish a child to give them up is likely to work the wrong way—reinforcing them—for such symptoms usually arise as a way of coping with the tension from other sources, tension which often is not obvious to the parent. Many of the tensions are based on the normal stresses of growing up. If parents' concern centers attention or anxiety on the symptom, it becomes set as a "habit" pattern, used instead of words to express feelings. Such habits cannot be given up by the child at will.

As mentioned earlier, a parent's first responsibility is to check out the symptom, to make sure there is no serious physiological cause. Then, the parent's role is to evaluate and understand the reasons behind the symptom. For children who are functioning well in other areas of life, and for whom there appears to be no real reason for concern about development in general, the best rule may be to wait and see whether they won't give up the symptom as they master the next stage of development. For the child who seems locked into a symptom which is serious enough to interfere with present or future adjustment, there are at least three courses open to the parent. The first is to try to let up on the other pressures in the child's life, to give him a better image of his own strengths. The second is to attempt to look beyond the symptom to the conflicts behind it. This is harder, and there are many reasons why parents cannot always understand a child. For example, they may be blinded to his conflicts for their own reasons, since his conflicts touch on their problems, too, and they may find it particularly hard to admit that the child has any problems at all. One of the most common sources of problems in a child is tension between parents. As soon as they admit to a difficulty in the child, they begin to blame each other for it. Of course, this increases the family tension and adds to the child's problem. In a preschool in Cambridge, Massachusetts, the teachers reported that they could predict which fathers were writing theses and which mothers were taking exams by the number of infections the children suffered. Even more obvious is the incidence of acute respiratory infections in small children just as their parents are about to go away on a trip, or when the family is about to make a move to another city. This simply may be a matter of lowered resistance which results from normal tension in a household.

One of the most difficult things to do at a time like this is to face the problem squarely and work together to solve it. I have spoken of some of the ways in which a parent can put into words the reasons behind the child's conflict, uncovering them for the child, and thereby helping him both to understand himself and to feel understood by his parents. When these efforts are not enough, or when the child may need to keep his parents out and cannot respond to their efforts, the third course open to parents is to seek outside help. Help can be in the form of an understanding teacher, physician, or guidance counselor.

A physician who is interested in the total child and his problems can be of invaluable help both in prevention and cure. Obtaining this kind of help is not always easy in this age of superspecialization, but it is surely worth seeking a physician who can work with the whole family. A pediatrician or a family doctor may be such a person. The first step in incorporating a doctor's help is to establish an open, confident, working relationship with him (or her). Bare your concerns and fears, and seek this professional's advice to help put your child's growth into perspective. As children grow, see that they develop a positive, trusting relationship with a doctor. He (or she) can act as an objective third party and confidant for the child. A doctor can make observations, see beneath the symptom to the reasons behind it, and even interpret these insights directly to the child. If there is a trusting relationship built up, all of this will mean a great deal to the sick child. If a child can have a direct relationship with the physician, not through his parents, this relationship may be even more effective in breaking the vicious cycle of psychosomatic symptoms and disease. It is always impressive to see the real relief with which a small child greets the doctor who comes to "fix him," while his anxious parents stand by. A 6-year-old looked at his doctor one day, as he stopped wheezing after a shot of adrenalin, and said, "If you'd been here sooner, I'd never have been wheezing." This kind of trust is worth a great deal of pediatric time and effort.

A physician who knows the family can be of real help to parents at such a time. Unfortunately many practitioners do not feel adequate in handling the task of giving advice, and hide behind "being too busy," or else reassure parents that "he'll grow out of it," when they know better. We would urge concerned parents to ask the doctor for a special consultation time and for his counsel as a knowledgeable, understanding person. If this help is not enough, ask for a consultation with a therapist who knows children's problems. In a medical center, ask for a psychiatric or psychological evaluation. On the strength of this, the child's problems may be uncovered so that the parents can help with them. The sooner this can be done, the less the problems have a chance to become ingrained, and the more amenable they are to treatment. Everyone in the family will profit, and after the initial difficulties of facing up to treatment are overcome, the rewards begin to be apparent to the child and everyone around. By seeking help early, a parent can help a child avoid possible psychosomatic problems later in life.

I hope these chapters, which each contain an issue of importance to children and to parents, will help show the ways to avoid conflict and tension. Childhood can be such an exciting and rewarding time for all. But over-conscientious, calvinistic parents look for things to be concerned about in their children's development. I know I spent far too many precious hours worrying about these deviations in my own children, at times when I could have been enjoying them and their progress instead. As outside pressures on parents increase, I would like to free up the "child time" for them to enjoy each other more. Parents who understand the child and their own inevitable emotional reactions are better able to take in their child's developmental progress.

The ideas expressed in this book have come from 30 years of pediatric practice in Cambridge, Massachusetts. I have been extremely fortunate in being able to share the problems of parents from a wide socioeconomic spread. At each visit, as they discussed their child's worrisome behavior, we had the opportunity to set that behavior in the context of the child's development, and to see what was behind their own reactions to the child. They worked harder than I in helping us all to understand it. As we had the chance in our continuing relationship to see the problems work themselves out, or more rarely to see them intensify and demand treatment, we came to share the understanding expressed in each of these chapters. Thus, the solutions offered herein are not mine but are gathered from a wealth of experiences shared with thousands of families who have lived in and moved out of Cambridge.

More recently, I have had the opportunity to explore some of these issues in parent-infant research at the Children's Hospital in Boston. Many outstanding researchers have shared their ideas with me and have listened to mine and helped me temper them. There is an increasingly large and powerful organization, the Society for Research in Child Development, composed of some 8,000 members (psychologists, sociologists, educators, nurses, physicians) who are all intensely involved in research with children. I have been an active member of this group, as have the researchers with whom I have worked.

In the past 13 years, I have had the opportunity to train pediatricians as fellows in a special program in behavioral pediatrics at the Harvard Medical School and Children's Hospital in Boston. Over these years I have shared ideas with some 40 exciting graduates of this program. Pediatrics is changing these days from a therapeutic, disease-oriented specialty to one which takes an important preventive and supportive role for young families. The Academy of Pediatrics now includes the Committee on Psychosocial Development of Children and Families. This committee is attempting to add normal child development training to the schooling of all pediatricians. Whereas, until now our training concerned diseases and their treatment exclusively, we at last are beginning to prepare young doctors and nurses for their roles in understanding and supporting normal development for children and families. It is an exciting time to be in pediatrics. These young physicians and nurses will see to it that the field changes to meet the needs of young families. Our training center in Boston brings physicians (and, more recently, nurses and psychologists) together for a two-year fellowship aimed at understanding normal child development and a family's role in fostering this. All of these trainees (about half are women and half are men) have already finished their full residency training in pediatrics or nursing, or already hold Ph.D.'s in psychology. They are mature and well equipped to understand the interactions between physical and psychological development. Their training consists of learning the extensive literature of research in child development, and of applying techniques for evaluating small children's emotional, cognitive, and motor development. They must learn how to assess small children in a way that allows them to understand how each child functions, and how to talk to troubled parents. We have found that one of the most powerfully effective techniques as we try to understand or to intervene in a stressed parent-child situation is the ability to "listen" to the child's behavior. By observing the child in play, under stress, and as he turns to his parents, one can develop insight into the pressures on that particular family. By bringing these reactions on the part of the child to the parents' attention, one can help them to a better understanding of their role in facing the problem with the child.

The nature of this listening can be seen in this example of a sleeping problem in a baby who was seen in our referral clinic by one of the pediatricians in training:

Lucy was a bright-eyed, curly-haired 7-month-old baby who was almost constantly in motion. Neither of her parents were able to hold her in their arms for long as she struggled to be "put down." She said "Dow" almost constantly, wriggling with strong determined efforts to get down, and if they ignored her, her protesting wails mounted to embarrass them and to force them to give her her way.

Lucy's mother and father were both physicians. Her father was 40 years old, a researcher in the chemistry of body fluids. Her mother, 37, was a successful internist who knew a great deal about adult medical diseases. Both were at the top of their professions when they made the decision to have this first baby after ten years of marriage. Mrs. Thomas reported earnestly how difficult for her it had been to make the decision: "I knew I was a success in one part of my life. Why take a chance on being a failure? And now I am one. Lucy never sleeps. She is up and down all night. She cannot sleep. She wakes up every three hours and we have to go to her. We have even tried to sleep with her, but then none of us can sleep. This way, we alternate— I go one time, my husband goes once, then I go the next time. But we are so tired all the time that I can't possibly go back to work. My husband can't do his work. I feel like a complete failure as a parent. Lucy dominates us and that's not the way it should be. What can we do?" Desperation was in her voice as she told this story.

Mr. Thomas nodded throughout his wife's plea for help and nodded enthusiastically as she posed her final question. He seemed in complete agreement with his wife, and said he felt as utterly helpless as she.

Meanwhile, Lucy hardly noticed them. She was actively cruising around the room. She crawled actively from one piece of furniture to another, pulling herself up on each one when she reached it. Her motor activity was precocious for her age, as she performed more like a 9- or 10-month old. All of this activity was rather driven and frantic. At one point, she toppled over and hit her head on the floor. Although both parents jumped to attend to her, Lucy hardly whimpered. When Mrs. Thomas tried to pick her up to comfort her, Lucy shrugged her off and crawled quickly away to explore in another part of the room.

"See, she acts as if she doesn't even need me. Here she is in a strange room, and she feels more at ease than I do. She doesn't even worry about you, and yet I'm nervous about exposing myself to you. I feel as if Lucy doesn't need me as a mother. Why did we decide to give up our lives to her?"

The anger at Lucy's competence was not well hidden, nor were Mrs. Thomas' feelings of helplessness and of disappointment. The pediatrician commented on the fact that these feelings must pervade their behavior toward Lucy at night when she woke them. Her father said, "She is so good at standing up in bed, that she comes half awake, gets up on the side of the crib, and starts screaming. We've tried to let her cry it out but she's stronger than we are. If we let her cry too long she just gets more worked up, and then we can never get her down to sleep. We are so angry and tired all the time that we can hardly face her day or night. Can you help us?"

These two (more senior) physician-parents were presenting their helplessness and desperation to a (younger) pediatrician-in-training. The younger physician, Dr. Fines, began to feel as helpless and anxious as the parents when they recounted the programs they'd already tried to get Lucy to sleep. As she explored the feelings of helplessness, she elicited from them the fact that Lucy had dominated them "from the first." She'd been an active fetus in the uterus. Her mother had hardly slept in the pregnancy's last three months, and already dreaded Lucy before her birth. When she arrived, Lucy was an active, extremely alert newborn. Both parents were awed by how perfect she was, how competent she seemed from the first day. Mrs. Thomas said, "She knew more about breastfeeding than I did, so I just followed her and we were successful. It has always been that way. If I did things her way, we were okay. But when she couldn't be satisfied, we fell apart." She looked at her husband, who nodded. "The first real crises began when Lucy was 3 weeks old and started fussing at the end of each day. She developed typical colic and we were frantic. Lucy's doctor, who is a good friend of ours, has been no help. He just says, 'She'll outgrow it.' 'If you calm down, so will she.' But she hasn't outgrown it and we can't calm down. She's stronger than we are."

As it became apparent that the struggle between them was not just a sleeping problem, but had invaded her feeding (she refused to be fed and they were already into feeding problems) and discipline (for they were unable to say "no" to her), as well as her day-and-night regulation, Dr. Fines commented that she saw this more as an inter-actional problem which now dominated their relationship. Both Thomases agreed. As if Lucy sensed the agreement, she crawled over to Dr. Fines to pull up at her lap. She put her arms out to be picked up by the young pediatrician. She lay her head against this young woman's shoulder as if she felt safe and could rest for a while. Mrs. Thomas commented with a slight glimmer of jealousy, "She knows you already."

Dr. Fines talked to them over the resting baby, to say, "I do see her as a wonderfully competent, even precocious baby. But she, too, is feeling the same desperation you are. She wants us to come to some resolution for her sake as well." Lucy's very behavior at that moment seemed to be a search for a more comforting situation than she had when she herself was in control. Her parents agreed with the younger physician that leaving it to Lucy was not comfortable for any of them. They began to discuss the elements that contributed to their feelings of helplessness. Her mother talked about Lucy's strong, de-termined, and demanding personality, which was balanced by their own feelings of inexperience. Behind this inexperience in mothering and fathering was the knowledge of their success in other parts of their lives. This aggravated their sense of helplessness, and even of angry desire for escape from a responsibility which they couldn't live up to. Dr. Fines wondered whether they remembered any experience with feeling helpless like this before. Such a memory might give them all some insight into how to work with this situation.

Mrs. Thomas fairly blurted out, "The reason I never wanted a baby was that I saw my mother try to take care of my little brother. She was at his mercy all the time. Although I was only 6 when he was born, I could see that she felt controlled by him. My father was scorn-ful of her and used to say 'Women are like that. They want to be dominated—even by a baby!' I hated him for that, and swore I'd never be such a woman. Then my brother, when he was only 4, said to my mother when she was dressed to go out one day, 'You stay home. You belong in the kitchen!' These two memories drove me to become a professional who was not 'in the kitchen.' Now I'm as much at Lucy's mercy as was my mother." With this outburst came tears, and Mrs. Thomas added as she finished, "I'd never put two and two together before, but I am repeating my mother's pattern, aren't I?"

Mr. Thomas was surprised and touched by his wife's outburst, which he followed with, "I didn't realize how much you need me to help you. I can be of more help than I've been. I, too, am following my family's patterns. My father never made a decision or helped at home, but left it all to my mother. I'm amazed at how passive I've been in all this. I think I've been secretly admiring Lucy's strength, but you tell us it's partly anxiety. I agree. We must work to help her."

After these insights into some of the issues behind the Thomas' feelings of helplessness, Dr. Fines felt empowered to talk about Lucy's needs. She described the need for discipline from parents that drives a child to a great deal of provocative behavior. Dr. Fines wondered whether her waking at night, her constant activity, and her refusal to be fed weren't in part attempts to elicit a clearer sense of her parents than they had been able to give her. Dr. Fines encouraged them to see their roles as more critically important. She pointed out the wonderful excitement and the charm of this baby, and credited them with having fed that in her. But she agreed with them that they all needed to work together to channel Lucy's energy and her intensely driving personality. They asked how they could do that.

As Dr. Fines began to try to give them specific instructions about discipline, and about letting her do more about her own sleeping pattern, it became obvious that the Thomases were not able to take in her instructions. Their eyes clouded and they looked away.

In our referral clinic, the physician trainee is being observed and backed up by a supervisor in the observation room, behind a one-way glass. When the history has been taken from the family, and the child assessed successfully, the trainee suggests that the parents take the baby for a snack, while the physician confers with his or her observing supervisor. During this break, the family has a chance to confer with each other and to be sure they've covered their concerns. The supervisor then can help the physician reach an understanding of the dynamics of the case, and to set out a plan for addressing the issues which are involved.

In this case it seemed that the Thomases were dominated by deeper concerns which were interfering with their ability to take advice about handling Lucy. Until these deeper conflicts were addressed, advice was ineffective. We were sure that they would have gotten such advice from earlier visits to their own physician. The fact that they couldn't follow it was a further indication of their ineffectual approach to Lucy. Although the two physicians could guess what lay behind their concerns it was necessary to explore them with the Thomases. To do so might require seeing each of them individually.

When they returned to the room after the break, Mr. Thomas was holding a sleeping Lucy in his arms. Dr. Fines began by recapitulating her earlier findings—that Lucy seemed well put together but anxious, and that her anxiety seemed to indicate that her parents needed to reevaluate their relationship with her. She seemed to need a more secure sense of limits. Mrs. Thomas seemed eager to talk about her relationship with Lucy.

As they talked, Mrs. Thomas began to tell about how gratified she'd been with Lucy, but how she felt she was reproducing her mother's ineffectualness. Somehow, until she spoke of it today, it hadn't been clear to her that she was really afraid of being like her mother. And yet, her mother had been admirable—"Perhaps I'm afraid I'm not enough like her, and I really want to be." At this point Dr. Fines assured Mrs. Thomas that she hadn't ruined her baby with her ambivalent feelings and that Lucy was doing very well developmentally.

Mr. Thomas assured his wife and the young pediatrician that he felt backed up to play a stronger role in supporting his wife. They asked Dr. Fines for specific advice on Lucy's sleeping (see Chapter 9). They listened intently and seemed to be trying to absorb each word of advice.

They gathered Lucy up very tenderly at the end of the session, and seemed less tentative as they left. Two weeks later they returned with broad smiles on their faces. They began to tell Dr. Fines how grateful they were to her. After she had helped them uncover some of the dynamics behind their feelings about parenting, they had begun to see their roles more clearly. Mr. Thomas had been able to become firm with Lucy when his wife needed him. He had begun to participate with Lucy morning and evening. "I'm no longer afraid of her," he said. Mrs. Thomas was a different, more confident person. She kept reiterating how free she felt: "I can be two people—a mother and my old self. It's like a miracle. Helping me see that I was running away, and that I needn't run has made it a miracle. Lucy is a changed girl. She knows how happy we are with her, and she doesn't need to tease us all the time. What fun we are all having. Lucy cried the first night; I went to her and said firmly, 'Go back to sleep.' She did, and I couldn't believe it. She was happier about sleeping through the night than I was. She's only a baby, I realized, and not the monster I'd come to fear. What a really wonderful feeling we have about her now."

This case was an easy one for a physician who was sensitive to the helplessness the conflicts in the parents engender. It was necessary that these conflicts be uncovered and understood. Many of them are common to other new parents unable to make the clear decisions necessary to effect a comfortable relationship with a child. A pediatrician can help by listening to the child, and by helping his parents work toward an understanding of their past relationships. Lucy's parents were able to handle their anxiety and to come to a dramatic reorganization with very little help. They seemed to understand right away that their old attitudes were dominating their behavior, and they were strong enough to search for and uncover some of the reasons behind these attitudes. As soon as Dr. Fines indicated that this work was necessary for any solution to the sleep and other problems with Lucy, they could understand and do the work necessary to reorganize their relationship. Of course it seemed almost too miraculous that they could do this in one morning, but their readiness, their desperation before they came made it possible. They were ripe for advice about handling sleep, feeding, and disciplinary problems.

I hope this kind of psychological pediatrics is the wave of the future. Work in our program at Children's Hospital has given me a chance to try out such an approach and to share my ideas and ways of thinking about parenting issues with these future pediatric leaders.

The topics in this book have been treated more briefly in my bimonthly articles in *Redbook* magazine over the past six years. My chapter on "Complaints with an Emotional Element" in the (Boston) Children's Medical Center's *Child Health Encyclopedia* (Delacorte, 1975) has been adapted for part of this introduction. If these chapters prove to be of help to parents, my gratitude goes to those trusting and cooperative families who have helped me write them.

PART ONE

LOVE AND FEARS

2
HOW BABIES
LEARN ABOUT LOVE

The most common questions with which young parents confront me in my pediatric practice are: "Am I doing the right things for my baby?" and "How will she know that she is loved?" The first question is generated by a desire to take all the right steps in childbearing at a time when our culture is no longer very sure of its goals—and at a time when there are no sure ways for parents to find out what these goals should be. The extended family is not around to help pass them on, and a huge number of childrearing experts have followed in Dr. Spock's single path to make it a maze for young parents: Should I stimulate my baby or not? Should I use positive reinforcement? Should I take parent effectiveness courses?

Perhaps the fact that there are so many different points of view is good in some ways. At least young parents needn't be burdened by the feeling that there is just one answer and that they can't find it. The wealth of conflicting sources of advice may press them to find their own solution, an individual one rather than a prepackaged one. I worry about joining the fray and offering one more bit of advice to already overloaded parents. However, what I would offer would not be specific advice. All I can recommend is: "Do what makes you and your baby feel the best and gives you the nicest time together." When confronted with that answer at a party, anyone who is searching for a simple answer immediately turns away from me and finds a new, more rewarding conversationalist. When a parent who is seriously searching for the answer asks me, I can work toward fuller advice. I urge parents to follow their own "best instincts"—made up of a combination of intuition, their own past experience, and what they can learn about the issues with which they and their child are coping. Such a solution, of course, is not a fail-safe; along with good periods there will be periods of conflict. The difficult times can be used for reevaluation and change. I don't think that *what* you do as a parent is nearly as important to the child as *how* you do it—and what feelings of caring go into it. In other words, the very fact that you care and are concerned about your baby is the most important message that she will receive.

But—how will she know that you care about her? Don't all parents care about their children? Don't all of them mean well, and still make serious mistakes in rearing their children? Probably they do, but the degree to which they are freed of their own problems and able to listen to the child's own needs may differ considerably. Caring enough to be able to look beyond one's own needs in order to be there when your child needs you is no small order. And to be really available may be a lot harder than it appears to be on the surface.

A DANCE OF LOVE

To understand this process, several of us at Children's Hospital in Boston have been studying the development of bonds between mothers and fathers and their infants in the first few months. Drs. Edward Tronick, Heidelise Als, and I have been trying to find a way to record and evaluate the beginning of emotional and intellectual development, on the premise that the important messages conveyed by a caring parent to the infant can be captured. We have been observing face-to-face play sessions in our laboratory. We know it is difficult for people to play with their babies while they are being filmed and we know that a lab is not a natural setting. So, we look at this as a somewhat stressful situation. Nevertheless, we find that there is a predictable pattern of behavior as the mother and father interact with the infant over the three-minute session. When we slow the tape down in order to analyse it, we find some remarkable things in all cases in which the parents are having a "good" time with their babies. And when they aren't (as in cases in which the baby is failing to thrive because the parent can't give the infant the nurturing she needs, or cases in which the baby is setting off negative feelings in the parent), we can see the failure very clearly.

The baby is placed in a reclining infant chair, on a table. The mother is instructed to sit in front of her and to talk or play without picking her up. When the mother first comes in, she usually starts to talk gently to the baby, to hold onto her legs or her buttocks as she first greets her, and then begins to talk to her. When the baby sees her, she greets her mother with a bright smile and pays an increased attention to her. For the next three minutes of the session they play with each other in a kind of rhythmic dance as they signal back and forth. The baby usually sets the rhythm as she looks at her mother, her face brightening, her hands and legs reaching out toward her gently, then smoothly curling back into herself. If you watch her eyes by slowing the film you can see that she smoothly alternates between being intensely interested in her mother's attempts to engage her, and a dulled-down look in her eyes as she tunes herself down. Often she looks to one side to "recover" from the intense looks her mother gives her. She is attending intensely then recovering in a gentle but definite rhythm, as if to protect her rather fragile, immature heart and lung systems from becoming overloaded. Since cycles of intense to dull moods are going on at a rate of four per minute, one can see them only in slow motion. What you do see on direct observation is a rather quiet, alert, soft-looking baby who is responding to her mother in a way that makes you feel good.

If you watch the mother on the film, you will see that she, too, is playing the game of cycling in and out. She looks at the baby most of the time, but she plays with her in rhythms—touching her, then pulling her hand back only to return to touch her again, often patting or rubbing rhythmically and in time with her. She smiles and vocalizes in a timing very much synchronized with the baby's. Her head bobs gently forward when she looks at her, and withdraws when she tunes her down. All of her rhythms and her advances are timed to the baby's attention cycles. Again, looking at her without the benefit of sloweddown film, what you see is that she looks gentle and smooth, and is softly playing vocal or facial "games" with her baby.

Underlying all of this rhythmic cycling of attention and recovery is a very important communication system called a "feedback" system. As mother and baby are locked into each other's signals and rhythms, they are feeding each other more than simple messages. They are saying to each other that they are really in touch, and the feeling of synchrony says to both of them, "We are really locked into each other."

My colleagues and I see this as the base for the baby's earliest emotional communication. In this way she learns by "feedback" about the world around her, as well as about herself. The subtle rhythm which is maintained by both mother and baby can be manipulated at any moment by either one. If the baby changes it by a smile, the chances are that her mother will smile back—and thus she learns about the effect of smiling—on those around her as well as on herself. The same goes for vocalizing, for making a reaching-out gesture to which the mother will respond in her way. In this reciprocal system, no one leads the other all the time. At one point, the baby may be setting the tone; at another it will be the mother. Each leads the other in an alternating system. At any moment, either one can turn the other off. This part of it is important to the baby, whose immature nervous system makes it necessary to be able to turn her mother off before she, the baby, gets overloaded with the excitement of too many messages from mother. So, both mother and baby have some control over this dialogue. The baby is learning about herself and her influence on an important "other" by her behavior. The mother is learning how to tune in to her baby's responses and subtle needs.

THE FATHER'S STYLE

We have found that the father sets up a different but predictable behavioral system with the baby. By the age of 3–4 weeks his rhythm with the baby is clear and differentiated from the one the mother and infant have developed together. Drs. Suzanne Dixon and Michael Yogman in the Child Development Unit at Boston Children's Hospital have found that fathers are more likely to use a playful approach, and to "jazz a baby up" by heightening the rhythm the baby sets. They tap different parts of her body in rhythmic games, they speak in more heightened rhythms, and they exaggerate facial expressions in ways that seem to say to the baby, "Now, let's play!" A small baby first watches quietly as she starts such a period with her father. Then she will hunch up her shoulders, look eager, and finally laugh out loud, bouncing up and down in her chair. So predictable is this pattern that we have found that a baby of 3 months will take on an expectant look, hunched shoulders, and will lean forward in her chair when she hears her father's voice. It is as if she knew that her father's presence would result in this special playful kind of communication. Fathers, in turn, learn to expect very early to see this playful attitude on the face and in the body of the baby, and they respond to it with an expected, playful attitude. Even when the father is the primary caregiver, the baby seems to save a special "play" track for her father, and a softer, smoother, less heightened set of rhythmic responses for her mother. These predictable patterns indicate the importance to each of the participants of having a known set of behavioral signals which say to each, "You're here and I'm with you!"

A POWERFUL SYSTEM

Within this feedback system, the infant learns about her universe. She learns who can respond with intimacy; she learns what behaviors from her will elicit a response; and she learns that when she sets the tone she will be engulfed in this wonderfully rewarding exchange. In this way, she learns about herself as a social human being very early. It is in this system that I think she first learns that she is what we call "being loved." If I could demonstrate this to mothers and fathers who ask me, "How will she know when she's loved?" I think they would know what I mean when I say, "Watch her and she'll tell you." For indeed you can see and feel for yourself when this rhythmic interaction is working.

This reciprocal system is at the heart of parenting. Being there when she needs you and showing her that you care is the parents' side of this communication system, the baby's chance to learn that she's loved. The reward for you as you enter into this intimate communication is that you will "know" when you are in touch with your baby. The underlying rhythm of attention-inattention is so compelling that it carries you along. The baby's response to each bid is so heightened that you will feel a glow as she smiles, vocalizes, or wriggles all over. At the end of it, as if she were saying to you, "It's your turn now," she will turn off her response to wait for yours. In such a period of play, the chances to learn about each other are endless.

In our research, we have demonstrated the power of this system by interrupting it briefly. We ask parents to present a perfectly still face instead of a responsive one. The baby can hardly believe it. She demonstrates how much she has learned to rely on this system by her repeated and prolonged efforts to recapture her parents' playful rhythmic behavior. She will grin, gurgle, reach forward, fall forward in her chair, all in an effort to mobilize her inactive parent. Finally, after a minute or so of this unresponsive behavior, the baby will turn away to watch her own hands, or to attempt to go to sleep in order to avoid the painful violation of an unresponsive parent. Having learned to expect play and communication, she is undone without it. A depressed or withdrawn parent can have a devastating effect upon a baby.

These reactions are strengths in a baby of 4–8 weeks of age. When the mother does brighten up to play with her in the usual manner, the baby redoubles her responses with obvious joy. In other words, a small infant who is loved expects a kind of responsiveness from each of her parents, and when she does not get this she has marvelous, strong ways of defending herself from the disappointment—at least temporarily. In these defensive periods, she well may be learning important coping mechanisms for future disappointments.

Another but important part of this intense signalling system is the capacity of the parents or the baby to put an end to it. I am convinced that limits are as important to a baby's learning about herself as are any other aspects of her world. If she spent all the time bathed in this reciprocal system without interruption, her day certainly would become too heightened or too flat and even boring. So, the limits on it are as important as the fact that it exists. The baby learns that she can participate in such a period of intense interaction, but that a necessary separation will follow. From this experience of separation, she will learn that she is a separate individual and can manage for herself, too. This system feeds her development, as does the frustration of terminating it and the experience of being left to herself. I am convinced that part of a parent's responsibility is to allow a baby opportunities for autonomy—to learn that when she reaches for and gets an object in front of her, it may be even more fulfilling than to have the object handed to her. There are times, in other words, when setting limits, saying "no," or even leaving the baby to find her own answer may also tell a baby that you love her.

In this way, the small infant learns early about loving and being loved. We can see this rhythmic softening and brightening in infants who are loved on the wards of Children's Hospital. We can also see its contrast—the staring, wide-eyed, nonrhythmic look of a baby who has not been loved. Wariness about social communication is coupled with a kind of hunger in such a 1- or 2-month-old baby. This ability of the infant to get into a rhythmic back-and-forth system of brightening, smiling, and cooing tells us whether she is nurtured enough at home.

HYPERSENSITIVE INFANTS

Nevertheless, there are infants who are difficult to nurture. As one attempts to rock them gently, they stiffen and arch away. As they are rocked, they have a series of body startles which result in inconsolable crying. If one looks in the face of such a baby or talks to her, she arches, looks frightened, and turns away. Every attempt to reach out for this kind of infant seems to result in negative responses. She cries for long inconsolable periods in the day. Social stimuli seems to turn her off but not on. What can a parent do to reach such a baby? Any caring parent will automatically blame herself for failure with such a baby. Mothers tell me that they *know* it is their fault. This very feeling of guilt and of inadequacy can build up to a feeling of helplessness and even of anger toward the baby: Will she ever accept me? What am I doing wrong? These feelings create anxiety and press a parent to redouble her efforts to reach the baby. In turn, the efforts overload the baby even more, and she turns off even more dramatically. The stage can be set for feelings of failure on both their parts—in the mother, a feeling of having failed as a parent, and in the baby, an expectation to fail in reaching others.

In order to try to understand this failing process, we have studied a group of babies who demonstrated what we saw as hypersensitivity to social stimuli even in the newborn nursery. In the noisy, overlit nursery, they lay with staring eyes, looking off into the distance and *frowning.* As we watched them, although they appeared to be awake, they seemed almost mesmerized and unavailable. If you talked gently to them, or touched them, or crooned to them, or rocked them, they looked more worried. Their frowns would deepen, their eyes become more glazed as they stared doggedly away. As one tried to get a "positive" response, their respirations would increase to become deep and regular. If one persisted, they often would turn actively away, their color would worsen, and they might even have a bowel movement or spit up. Normal social stimuli seemed to be too much for these babies from the start. The kind of things which any well-meaning parent might do to capture a response from these babies brought stiffening, turning away, and withdrawal.

These babies were likely to be long and lean, slightly dryskinned, with their pinched faces resembling little old people. They might have been somewhat depleted in the uterus for no predictable or explainable reason. Although undernourished women, heavy smokers, drinkers, or addicted women do produce babies like this, for many of these babies there is no available explanation. A mother who is handed such a baby will automatically feel this behavior is her fault. Since many of these babies are not too underweight (6–6-½ pounds) and are not premature, the medical staff treats them as normal and leads the parent to expect normal behavior. But this kind of responsiveness is not normal and a parent unconsciously knows it. The ingredients for failure to create a loving interaction are in the baby. The parent feels they are in her handling, and the two can be off to a rather doomed start.

When we realized that these babies were demonstrating a kind of hypersensitivity as newborns, it began to explain other behaviors we saw in these babies. Their ability to control their state of consciousness was not as effective as it was in most full-term babies. Most such babies would come from sleep slowly and be reachable for interaction for a while; even in crying they could be reached temporarily by a voice or by holding and rocking them. They would give one the feedback of having done the right thing for them. Yet not these hypersensitive infants! They could either sleep or stay unavailable in a dull, drowsing state or they would snap right into crying in a short period. In any of these three states, they were unavailable. Their periods of availability for being responsive to their new parents were very short and unpredictable. They would fly off into unavailable screaming or frowning sleep before a parent could set up a feedback system for interaction. These were already unrewarding newborns. If one fed them, they ate greedily but often spat it up. If you tried to play with them at feeding times, they overreacted with their gastrointestinal tracts. Some had colic and diarrhea. From the first three weeks, they literally slept and ate and then cried for long, inconsolable times, until they were at least 12 weeks old.

As we studied them and listened to their distraught parents, we began to reassess the job of caregiving they needed. In order not to set them off immediately, we found we must either touch *or* hold *or* look at *or* talk to them, but not all at once. If we adjusted whatever we did to them by cutting down on the rhythm, the quality, and the intensity of the stimulus, so that it was not only gentle but very low-keyed, we could see that the baby's initial shudder and stiffening response was followed by a relaxation and a kind of soft crying and turning to take in the stimulus. Although the response was extremely subtle and almost undecipherable, it was no longer avoidant or negative. One could see that the baby could accept one stimulus at a time, but not more than one. And even that stimulus had to be turned down to her limits. We had found a way to reach her that did not immediately turn her off! As we learned to respect her inordinately low threshold for taking in stimuli, and the cost to her of organizing her responses to the stimulus, we began to understand her better. We could see that she could settle down slowly to take in and respond to an auditory *or* visual *or* tactile stimulus, *or* the kinesthetic stimulus of being picked up or rocked. But she could respond only to one of these at a time without overreacting and losing the organization which was so difficult for her.

Since we have begun to understand these infants, we have been able to demonstrate this hypersensitive, overreactive behavior to their parents. Instead of feeling helpless and ineffectual with their babies, they can change their approach, slow down, cut down on stimuli around such a baby, and deal with her in a low-keyed way. Swaddling them helps at times. Using a pacifier or teaching them to suck on their own thumbs may help them gain a kind of control system of their own. Feeding them in a quiet, darkened room with as little stimuli around them as possible can also be a help. Keeping their days and nights on a regular, predictable schedule and cutting down on too much activity is a help to both these babies and their parents.

These hypersensitive babies are at one extreme end of a spectrum of difficult-to-understand infants. Parents must exercise great sensitivity to be able to nurture them successfully. Parents who had expected a lovely, calm, easy-to-reach baby must adapt their rhythms, their level of stimuli, their whole day-and-night cycle to meet these babies' needs. It is a great challenge. To teach these babies to take in and respond to stimuli without losing control over themselves can be an enormous task. But when such a baby is reached and can learn over time how to manage her environment for herself, she is on her way to a successful future.

If such a baby is not reached in infancy, she will be likely to grow up with the same hypersensitive overreactions that she is born with. For example, if she shudders and turns away from each bit of information from her environment because it is too much for her sensitive nervous system, she will not be able to learn to integrate information which is important to her progress. Meanwhile, her family will see this "turning away" behavior as an indication that they are failures with her. Instead of looking for what kind of stimuli she might be able to utilize, they are too caught up in their natural concern for being perfect parents. They sense the failure developing between them and pull away from her, because they care so much. In the process of turning away, they offer her less and less opportunity for learning how to deal with her overly sensitive nervous system. Thus, fewer and fewer opportunities for interaction are coupled with the continuing failure of being unable to participate in enjoyable interactions when they do occur. The parents' frustration begins to convey itself to the baby. They almost are bound to treat her in a way that makes her sense herself as a failure. Her own behavior will begin to reflect this sense of failure. She will act in ways that create distress around her. She will overreact and begin to cry, or to turn away. She will react with clumsiness or provocativeness as time goes on. She will fall into furniture and demonstrate an insensitivity to it. Her behavior will elicit negative disapproval more than reward from her parents. An expectation to fail begins in infancy and is reinforced by parents whose caring behavior is unrewarded. A failure system develops. Only an understanding of the mechanisms of a hypersensitive nervous system in the baby might prevent this. These are difficult infants for even the most well-intentioned parents.

With every baby, the parents' main job is to establish a loving environment which adapts itself to the rhythms and responses of the individual infant, so that she can learn about herself. Within the nurturant envelope (called *love*) provided by a (loving) parent, she will learn how to react, interact, and what to do to regain control when she overreacts. This is a big job for both. Fortunately, such loving brings great response from most small babies, so that parents feel when they are on the right track and can feel rewarded for their efforts.

In order to feel loved, a person must love herself. For this, she must have strong feelings of autonomy, of being able to deal with frustration, of being able to incorporate in herself the firm limits of a caring environment. So a parent who loves must also convey these limits. This may seem like a negative message, unless it is seen as a way of helping the child learn *all* about herself and the world. She must learn that she is loved, but that sometimes a parent must say, "Now you've gone too far." Helping her learn this can be love, too.

3
FEARS IN
SMALL CHILDREN

Expressing fears can be one way for a child to cry for help. They strike a sensitive note in parents and generally produce a comforting reaction. If they occur often enough, they may call attention to a more deep-seated insecurity in the child, and parents then may be forced to eliminate unnecessary pressures and stresses on the child. In this way fears in children serve a double purpose.

Fears and being fearful are a normal part of childhood. They express the child's need for dependency and occur especially at certain times in a child's development. Nearly always they accompany a rapid spurt in one or more areas of development—in the intellectual, emotional, or motor spheres.

STRANGER ANXIETY

A child's first fears may be expressed as a heightened sensitivity to strangers, which crops up at several expectable points in the first year. Peaks of stranger awareness and the fear of strangers are the first evidence in babies of their increasing ability to distinguish the important people in their lives. Learning to tell mother from father and from "others" is a major job of infants, and it starts early. For example, our research in the Child Development Unit at Boston Children's Hospital

33

(with Drs. Michael Yogman, Suzanne Dixon, Heidelise Als, and Edward Tronick) has confirmed that by the age of 4–6 weeks, babies recognize fathers and behave differently with them than with mothers or with strangers. They also can tell strangers as early as this. By 4 months they become increasingly wary of whoever is not mother or father and try to avoid close contact with that outside person. Even a familiar "other" may create anxiety. It is at this very stage of development that a baby is becoming acutely aware of all new things in his environment. All sights and sounds suddenly seem more important. This awareness accompanies a well-recognized cognitive spurt at 4 months.

I often have been told, for example, that 4-month-old babies will look over a mother's sister or a father's brother very carefully. After such a lengthy assessment, the baby will begin to cry relentlessly if he is picked up by this familiar "stranger." Not until his mother or father takes him back will he stop crying. Is this "fear" on the baby's part? It represents the dawning awareness of very slight but important differences. If a familiar grandmother or grandfather looks him in the face at this age, he will break down into loud, protesting wailing.

In my office I find that 5-month-old babies may grin at me and gurgle at me across my desk but that when I come too near or look at them too closely, they break down in sobbing. This seems to me to show that at 5 months eye-to-eye and close contact is more important than it was previously. It must now be saved by the infant for very important and familiar persons such as mother and father. The "fear" appears at a time when the child's awareness of differences, and of their importance, is at a new peak.

This first peak of awareness is followed by an even more violent stage of stranger anxiety at 8 months. At this age one can expect a baby to be wary of all strange places and most strange people. As long as he can cling to and can hide his face in his mother's clothing, he can manage a new situation. But if one takes him out of his mother's arms or comes up too abruptly, this will set him off. The loud noise of sudden laughter or the direct confrontation of eye-to-eye contact in a strange situation will send him off into self-protective wailing. This second stage of fearfulness also parallels an increased awareness of his usual familiar surroundings, and it accompanies a new ability to explore these surroundings. The baby is just learning to crawl, to get around by himself, to leave his mother's base; he seems to demand the same environment for this exploration, and any change is too complicated for him at this time. He is learning more and more about "object permanence." In other words, when things or people are out of sight, they have not stopped existing and can be retrieved. He is just learning that he can follow his mother around a corner. He has new control over whether familiar persons and things disappear or not. Hence he wants to exercise that control in familiar surroundings and with familiar persons. New situations and new persons threaten this control. Harriet Reingold of North Carolina has pointed out that a baby will not be anxious if he can have the time and the control to approach the stranger himself. It is only when this is threatened by the stranger approaching that he breaks down with anxiety and fearfulness. The rapid increases in a child's understanding and in his wish to maintain control create an imbalance and make him more vulnerable to change, to fear of strangers, and to strange situations.

At 1 year of age these same imbalances create new turmoil. For a few months the baby may have been tranquil about strangers and strange situations. But when he stands, is learning to walk, and is cruising around the house, he becomes sensitive to and fearful of change all over again. He hates being taken to a new house. He worries about being approached by adults other than his parents. He won't let his mother and father out of his sight. When they walk out of the room or when they turn their backs on him, he collapses in tears. It is no surprise that his awareness of "person permanence" has increased with his new mobility. At this age the issue behind a child's "fears" again seems to be that of control. He wants to be the one to leave; he wants to be the one who walks away or turns his back. A sense of control allows the baby to make choices: Will I walk away? Will I let my parent go? Losing control seems to threaten all his newly found motor skills and the sensitivity that goes with them.

With these struggles during the day, one can expect turmoil at night. The baby may wake up screaming two or three times a night at this age. Standing in his crib, only half awake, he sobs as if terrified by a bad dream.

These periods of awakening come at this time for good reasons. The child's new activities lead to all sorts of unresolved experiences. The frustration left over from the day expresses itself at night, and the fears are a cry for help. Nighttime fears at the end of the first year are an expectable reaction to the excitement of learning so many new things.

TURMOIL IN THE SECOND YEAR

The next peaking of fears may be at the end of the second year or in the first half of the third. The child may suddenly become afraid of loud noises—fire engines, vacuum cleaners, the washing machine. A burst of laughter from an old friend may set him off. Rushing him into a new situation too quickly may produce a fearful reaction rather than the usual temper tantrum. Again, let's look for the underlying mechanisms.

Turmoil is at its peak at the age of 2–2-1/2 years. A child is caught between yes and no, in or out, will I or won't I. Often, no one around the child even cares about which alternative is chosen, but *he does*— and he cares so much that he can't handle the turmoil. Loud sounds or sudden changes set off an abrupt awareness of the inner turmoil he is experiencing and his lack of control over it. Crying in protest is a way to gain support. Tantrums act as a release at such times. An outgoing, expressive child who has been successful at expressing himself with tantrums may use them to express fear also. A quiet, internalized child may express fear in more subtle ways as he seeks adult backup. In either event, fears come as a real surprise to parents. They must be recognized as part of a new phase in development.

When fears begin to surface, a parent must evaluate the situation and respond appropriately. In the outgoing, aggressively expressive child, fears may find more than one outlet, and he will in all likelihood be able to handle his turmoil alone. If, on the other hand, the child is the quiet sort who finds it difficult to express himself, fears can be taken as an occasion for parents to begin to draw him out, to help him to express himself more openly.

FEARS AND AGGRESSION

By 3-1/2 or 4 years of age, fears accompany the beginning of normal aggression. Most children begin to have feelings of aggression at this age as part of growing up and of trying themselves out. The psychoanalyst Erik Erikson has described how aggressive feelings surface at 4 or 5 years. But, before they can be acknowledged or acted upon, they are boiling around inside. A child begins to experience complicated feelings when he sees a toy gun or when he imagines himself using one. When he wants to lash out at someone but dares not, there aren't too many ways to handle the feelings that keep coming to the surface. Fears help to keep them in check. Selma Fraiberg's wonderful book, *The Magic Years,** has outlined for parents some of the sources and the evolution of these fears in 3–6-year-olds. All parents of children in this age group should read it.

---

*New York: Charles Scribner's Sons, 1959.

An example from my practice illustrates this type of fear: "My 3-1/2-year-old is suddenly afraid of everything. He's fearful of fire engines and loud noises. He's especially afraid of the dark and of going to bed alone. When my husband and I leave the house, he has to know where we are going, why, and who we will be with—and he likes to hear me tell him over and over. It reminds me of how frightened I used to feel when I was an adolescent and had to go to a dance or a party all alone. He seems to feel so isolated from us. Is he all right? What have I done to make him so worried?"

As Mrs. Holmes talked earnestly, Alfred watched her with concern in his big gray eyes. Before she'd gotten onto this subject, he'd been noisily and demonstratively playing in my examining room, crashing the trucks into each other and strutting around with a yard-stick stuck over one shoulder as if it were a gun. He marched in almost goosestep precision, saying, "one, two, one, two" so loudly that we'd had to shut him up. As I watched him act out this military display, I remembered a conversation his parents and I had once had about guns for little boys. Mr. and Mrs. Holmes were pacifists and did not want Alfred to have guns or toys that symbolized aggression. So I was sensitive to Mrs. Holmes' embarrassment when she stopped Alfred's play and interfered with what she recognized as his showing off for me. She apologized briefly to me by saying, "He must have learned that from television."

Before this rather provocative bit of behavior, I recalled that Alfred, who is a sturdy, noisy little boy, had shouted, "Hi, Doc!" when he saw me and rushed gaily into my office to "attack" my toy corner. So delightful and outgoing was his greeting, that it was hard for me to see Alfred as a very worried child. Certainly the most critical interpretation one could make of his behavior was that through his aggressive play he was working out his feelings about being in a doctor's office where he was vulnerable and open to attack. It was clear to me that all of this outward bravado was hiding anxiety which, under the circumstances, was appropriate.

Routine exams, when they are not coupled with shots or other traumatic events, are a good chance for me to see how a child is navigating. Since coming to see me is bound to be a stressful situation, I always watch to see whether the child is tense or worried as he comes into my office and how he handles his natural concern about the visit.

My patients know that I like them and that I have a reward for them at the end of each visit. But they also know I will ask their mothers or fathers about them—and they do have worries about our talking about them. They usually listen carefully to what their parents tell me. Anything "wrong" is quickly equated in their minds with being bad, and if they've had an illness or a physical problem, they equate it with being naughty in my eyes. I need to reassure them from time to time that I don't think that way.

They also know they will have to undress and be examined. Whether or not they see this as painful is not the point. They do see it as intrusive and as an invasion of their personal space. Moreover, at Alfred's age, children are already afraid that I might find something wrong, which will need "fixing." Of course they equate the visit with shots, and they are naturally worried about being hurt. Children usually focus all their concerns on the issue of injections and inevitably ask as they enter my room, "Do I need a shot?" The degree to which they can settle down after I assure them that they don't gives me a measure of their general level of anxiety when confronting other kinds of stressful situations.

I was watching Alfred for anxiety as he undressed himself, trying to see how dependent he was, how reluctant he was to leave his mother's side, and how he dealt with my reassurances about being examined. He seemed easy about all this and trustingly allowed me to lift him up on my examining table. He lay down calmly on the table and didn't wince as I examined him. Even when I pulled down his underpants to examine his genitals, he seemed at ease with me.

Alfred wasn't upset at all, I felt. In fact, he seemed wonderfully assured about me. He used both his independence and dependence on his mother in an appropriate way. I felt he was an easy little boy and not unusually anxious at all. Hence, it was easy for me to allay Mrs. Holmes' worries about him and to reassure her that there was nothing wrong in her mothering.

I realized, though, that the questions Mrs. Holmes had asked reflected concerns about fears in small children that are universal. In order for her not to reinforce Alfred's fears, she would need an understanding of what was behind them.

I tried to explain to her that I thought Alfred's fears represented a period of rapidly learning about himself. He was learning what it was like to feel aggressive. This period in children's lives always demands an extra adjustment. How will he learn to control his aggression? Learning about himself at such a time carries with it a price. As they become aware of new feelings, children fall into a kind of imbalance in which they may become temporarily oversensitive to things and events around them. This increased sensitivity is likely to show up in the form of fearfulness or of expressed fears. These are an expression of the normal anxiety that goes with the reshuffling of one's ideas and awareness of aggressive feelings. A child with fears can be seen as asking for help from those around him—help to see the limits of the new feelings as well as the limits of his own capacity to deal with the situation.

This, I explained to Mrs. Holmes, was the function fears were serving for Alfred—they were helping him learn to control his aggression. I assured her that Alfred was an open little boy who could tease me, could let his aggressive feelings out in play with his toys, with his brothers, and by being naughty with his mother. But the emotional cost was bound to be great, and he was bound to feel guilty about it. Acknowledgment of guilty feelings and feelings of turmoil seems too risky, so he expresses himself in his fears. His fear allowed him to regress to a more helpless state, through which he could gather in longed-for attention from his parents. As he did this, he projected all of these frightening aggressive feelings on something outside of himself. He then could be afraid of aggression in others around him.

I couldn't resist the opportunity to urge her to stop trying to control Alfred's aggressive behavior, for that was reinforcing his fears. Playing with sticks as guns is a natural form of aggressive play at this age, and I was pretty certain that she'd only shove his aggressive feelings under by prohibiting such play. This, in turn, would only accentuate his fears. I urged her to think of acceptable aggressive play that he could learn which might serve the same purpose he was after—of learning about himself. Fears, I could reassure her, were serving a major developmental purpose for Alfred.

The danger is that a parent may overreact at such a hint. Just as Mrs. Holmes had, parents are likely to feel that such fears are reflecting deeper disturbances. When they appear, the parent's confidence in a child's healthy development may be shaken at a time when he needs that confidence the most. By taking the fears more seriously than they deserve, parents can reinforce them. This is particularly true if the child's fears remind them of their own past fears. Whenever they can meet fears with understanding sympathy and explain the reality of them in a reassuring way, the child may well be reassured. But if he listens and still has fears, the parents often become frustrated and increase the child's fearfulness. It is important for parents to realize at this point that their responsibility is not so much to rid their child of his struggle as to be an anchor for him. The very power of these fears reflects the importance of the mechanisms underlying them.

FACING FEARS

Because parents feel that their child's fears are due to intense internal conflicts or pressure, they may let up on discipline. They may bend over backward to please and pamper him. This can serve to make things worse. Unless they continue to offer the security of customary limits, he may indeed become frightened of himself—of his provocativeness, of his acting out. Limits—even if he doesn't like them at the time—may help him resolve the issues underlying the fears. It is still the child's task to resolve his fears, but he can resolve them better with a strong, reassuring backup from his parents.

In order to help their boy or girl regain confidence, parents may find that they have to face the fears directly with the child. If their daughter is worried about dogs, for example, she may need to be told more about dogs. She may need to know that dogs bark because they want to say "hello" and that they also bark to say "stay away." The parent might say "Let's learn together about dogs. Let's find out what a dog is trying to say. Is he wagging his tail? Do we dare pet him?" The real issue, however, is not a cognitive one. That is, the fears will probably not simply disappear once the child has acquired some information about the fearful object. The child also needs to know that it is okay to feel frightened of the dog's barking. She needs to know she can handle her fears.

After the fears are faced directly, the child still will need to understand his underlying feelings. It is no coincidence that a small child with a new baby in the house begins to be fearful. His feelings about the competition from the baby are sure to stir up angry and aggressive wishes. They will surface as fears when the child tries to hold in all of the negative feelings.

The oedipal feelings about a father which a boy is bound to have, the competitive feelings with her mother which a 4- or 5-year-old girl will experience, are too painful to be faced directly. Instead, fantasies of monsters in the closet will come to the boy at night. The little girl will wake up dreaming of witches who devour little girls or waft them away from their families. Thus, the guilt which accompanies forbidden desires has an outlet. It is projected onto a "monster" or a "witch" which can be gotten rid of by the parents' protection.

Fears and aggressive dreams are an expression of healthy development in the 4–6-year-old child. If parents respect them and are reassuring and protective, they can help the child learn about this phase of development in himself. To attempt to suppress or rid the child of aggression would be a tragic mistake. Adolescents who act out their aggressive feelings have too often been repressed at these earlier ages. It is far more preferable to help a child learn about acceptable ways for handling aggressive feelings. "See how Daddy behaves when he's upset or angry? He fusses at all of us, then he goes out to cut the lawn, and then he feels all better." "Mommy just gets mad inside, and that's not so good. When I get mad and then get over it and say, 'I'm sorry,' it's a lot easier on you, and I feel better too." These are statements which might give the child permission to identify with the family's ways of handling anger and aggressive feelings. These are ages when learning about sports or about how to handle competitive feelings can be particularly productive.

GUIDELINES

When a child is having fears, I would recommend the following:

1. First, see the fears as part of a normal spurt in development. In an older child the fears may accompany adjustment to a stress at school or at home. Or they may occur at times when the child is trying to deal with aggressive or competitive feelings. If parents look on fears this way, they can be less frightened of the symptoms in the child and lessen the anxiety around this symptom.

2. Offer the child reassurance about himself as well as (more directly) about the feared objects. Try to face them honestly and directly, but don't expect reassurance to allay them. A deeper understanding of why he may be fearful is the ultimate goal, but it may be hard to put into words. Often it is better expressed indirectly in ways that give the child permission to act out aggression or to verbalize anxieties and competitive feelings. Giving him acceptable ways to be aggressive and reassuring him about them may help a lot.

3. Do not let up on discipline and limits, but let the child know all over again the reason for the limits and how they help control the very feelings he may be fearful of. Congratulate him openly when he can conform to these limits and be patiently understanding when he can't. Let him know from you that it is a learning process which takes time. No one really likes to learn these limits.

4. Make the child aware of acceptable outlets for the negative or aggressive feelings. Talk openly of how other members of the family or of how friends he cares about handle their aggressive

feelings. Introduce sports and other acceptable ways for expressing these normally developing emotions.

5.   Help the child begin to express himself and to understand why he feels these negative, angry, and aggressive feelings. In doing so, you will be establishing invaluable patterns for sharing the inevitable turmoils of later periods, of adolescence, etc. Fears can be seen as a window into the inevitable periods of adjustment which all small children must go through.

4

WHEN A CHILD IS SAD

Being sad is very different for a child from crying. Crying is an active, protesting state, whereas being sad is a passive, low-keyed one. Crying can serve many purposes—anger, protest, a call for help, or just letting off steam at the end of the day (see the chapter on crying in my earlier book, *Doctor and Child*). After the crying period is over, the emergency will have been met, someone is likely to have responded, and everyone feels better. Life can be resumed. Not so with sadness. Sadness is a more prolonged state for the child. She is likely to respond to this feeling with little physical activity and few bodily changes. The depressed feelings do not express themselves or get alleviated easily. Since these feelings cannot be changed right away, they are likely to be frightening to parents. Parents may easily overreact, trying to push the child out of her "mood," or they may try to ignore it in her. Neither approach is likely to work for more than temporary periods. Sadness in a child is likely to represent a real cry for help.

How does a parent evaluate periods of sadness, and help the child pull out of them? First of all, I would suggest that their timing should be considered. Do these periods come at a time when there are real and understandable reasons for sadness? Have there been events which the child might find difficult to understand or to handle?

If so, there is already a better chance of helping the child recognize the reasons behind her sadness.

The next question I would ask would be, "How entrenched are these periods?" Is the child unreachable or can she cheer up when interesting events occur? If the former is true, it is a measure of how deeply affected she may be. But the fact that she can be cheered up or jostled out of her sadness needn't be a reason to ignore the mood, for it may well be an indication of things that deserve attention.

Finally, how much does this sadness invade other areas of the child's life, especially her relationships with others? Does it keep her from wanting to play with her friends, or do her friends shun her because she is sad? Do you feel sad when you are around her? All of these would be indications of the extent to which her sadness was affecting her, and could be used as guidelines in deciding how much should be done about it.

SADNESS AND LOSS

Most often, sadness is not a serious symptom, nor a lasting one. Being sad is a common experience in childhood. Parents wish they could prevent these periods for their children, but they can't. By the age of 3, a child already can understand and worry about the absence of a parent, the loss of an important person or a pet. The kind of loneliness or depression which follows a separation is comparable to that experienced by all of us as adults.

A 3-1/2-year old boy was in my office recently, dragging his rattly, but obviously beloved truck on a tattered string. When the string broke on a doorsill, he started to weep. I was struck with the sadness in his weeping. It was quite different from the protesting cry that I might have expected. I commented on it to his mother, who agreed with my observation. She said, "Danny hasn't been the same lately. His grandmother and grandfather were here for a month. They gave him such a great time that when they left, he acted as if the bottom had dropped out of his world. He went into their room several times a day looking for them, and called them his "best family." He even walked differently after they left and all his chipperness and spunk seems to have left him. I pray for him to have a temper tantrum again. He is so unhappy that everything gets to him and he won't fight back. The cat inadvertently scratched him and he wept just like this. That kind of sad weeping gets to me and I want to cry with him. Before this he would have gone after the cat and pulled her tail to pay her back. What can I do for him? I want my old Danny back. I'm so worried that I don't dare even mention his grandparents to him. When I do he just looks reproachfully at me like I sent them away. I didn't, of course. I miss them, too."

We talked about the good things in all of this—that Danny had begun to care so much about people other than his parents, that he could really miss them. Had he had any other real losses? His mother remembered he had had sad periods whenever his father went on a business trip, but these passed each time, and his mother tended to ignore them. Then, she remembered that they had lost their dog a few months ago. Since she didn't know how to deal with it, she had just hoped Danny would not miss him. They got the cat to replace him. Danny hadn't ever mentioned the dog or hadn't asked where he had gone. He had ignored the cat at first, but then he had begun to tease it and pull its tail. She had reprimanded him for torturing the cat, and he had retreated into a kind of sadness, she remembered. "Then of course," she said, "there is his new baby sister. He may be angry with her, but he has never shown that either. He seems to really like her. But I am pretty busy with her and he may miss time with me. It never really occurred to me—but his grandparents did take up a lot of slack with him whenever I was busy with her. I never put all of this together before, but it is obvious that Danny has had a lot to cope with recently."

In a very few minutes, Mrs. Gamble had laid out three layers of reasons why Danny might be sad. The new baby sister and the "loss" of at least a part of his mother was a first and very important layer. His father's trips away worried him, but everyone expected him to cope and he did. Then his beloved dog disappeared. His inability even to talk or ask about him meant to me that he had been bottling up some pretty heavy questions and feelings about loss in general. His mother's inability to face them with him had helped to keep them bottled up. The grandparents' visit probably brought all of them out into focus, and gave Danny a kind of permission to bring his feelings of loss to the surface. The sadness he expressed in my office seemed to me and to his mother to represent an appeal—for a chance to speak out and explore some of these losses. She felt guilty that she had not faced them with him before. I pointed out that even if she had faced each of them more openly they would have hit him. But she could help him to understand them better. Mrs. Gamble saw that now she had the opportunity to go back over these losses with him and to talk about each one in turn. In this way, she could unravel all the layers of his sadness. If she could do this successfully, she could help him understand and deal with them. Most of all, she could help him understand his own feelings.

Sadness is a symptom which needn't be avoided, and can't be. One of the most fascinating things about children to me is their economy. They can cope beautifully through a family crisis, asking for very little from their parents while the family's stress is high. Then, when it is safe and when parents have revived again and have enough energy, they can make a bid for the needed attention. Sadness represents just such a bid. Very often it harks back to a former loss or an earlier experience which was overwhelming at the time but repressed. When it surfaces, it is not too late to go back with the child in memory, to sort out the experiences and to relive them with her. In this way, she learns about herself and about her own ability to handle a painful experience. She is learning for future experience. At a safe time after such an experience of loss, she learns how to use memory and to put her experience into words. The experience of sharing losses with parents in early childhood can shore up a child to face the inevitable losses and disappointments that are in the fabric of life. If faced openly, sadness can help families become stronger and more able to handle painful feelings.

When there is a loss in the family, parents often are too caught up in their own grieving to offer much comfort for the child. Even the loss of the dog closed the Gambles off from each other. With any more significant loss, they'd have withdrawn even more, leaving Danny pretty isolated in his grief. Parents may need time to themselves to grieve. A child is bound to identify with their grief, to be both frightened and overwhelmed by it. However, she may go cheerfully on, using defenses, such as denial, to help get through. She may play normally with her toys and playmates. She may try to cheer up her parents. Later, her feelings may surface as bad dreams or nightmares or as sadness. It may occur so much later that the parents, recovered by now, will have difficulty in associating her behavior to the past event. But this symptom represents the cost of denying grief, or other such defenses, while parents are relatively unavailable.

It would be too bad if parents let themselves feel too guilty when this happens—when their child's sadness appears later and they realize that she, too, has suffered. For then they might not take advantage of the opportunity offered. Sadness is a plea for communication and for help. Learning about grieving, how to handle it, how to turn to people whom one trusts is a major job of each child and of each parent. Learning, even in childhood, that one can lose another, can miss them, can mourn and feel devastated, but can then recover is a great step.

Mrs. Gamble will be able to offer Danny such an opportunity. The experience of turning to his parents and being heard will teach him a great deal. At the same time, the parents will have the chance to examine their deep-seated beliefs about loss. They can reevaluate their own ways of coping with grief, and then share these important strengths with the child.

LOOKING BEHIND SADNESS

Sometimes sadness is not so much a direct response to loss as it is a way of handling other kinds of feelings. Feelings of inadequacy often surface in this manner. If a child's attempts to deal with his world are constantly unsuccessful, she may well become depressed underneath and sad on the surface.

During a visit with her 4-year-old, Mrs. Ransom asked if she could speak to me privately about her 9-year-old. At the end of the younger child's visit, I let him go out to play on the rocking horses in my waiting room. Mrs. Ransom is a tall, competent woman who has been a grade-school teacher in the past, and who consults for an educational firm at present. She resigned from teaching to raise her four children, but has managed to keep her consulting job going very successfully. She has taken deserved pride in her four great children headed by the 9-year-old, Matthew. As she spoke, I sensed deep concern in her voice. "He's so sad these days. He can't seem to perk up for anything. He even talks about killing himself, and that just frightens us to death. I can remember too well having feelings like that when I was little. He always has been such a happy child, and so competent. He had friends, but now they don't want to come over because he mopes around while they are there. His schoolwork and his love for sports are suffering, and his father and I are at our wits' end. Can you help us?"

This frightened me, too, for I don't hear stories like this very often. It is surprising that more children don't get depressed, but they rarely talk like this except in short bursts. All children go through days of feeling lonely or disappointed or angry or deserted enough to feel very sad. All of them want to punish the world around them for their sadness. And, I suspect, most of them have had the fantasy that the most effective punishment would be to kill themselves. I know that as a child I thought several times of punishing my parents for real or imagined slights by doing myself in. But the occasions of sadness were transient, and the reality of suicide pretty frightening. And yet I remember those feelings and could identify with Mrs. Ransom's concern about Matt's continued depression. The fact that it was deep enough and long-lasting enough to affect his friendships and his schoolwork worried me most. A transient period of feeling sorry for himself, in which he made life tough for his parents, would be commonplace and expectable. But when such a mood invades his other relationships and interferes with his entire life, it represents a more serious underlying problem. Whenever I am not sure whether a child is really troubled or not, I look at his peers' reactions to him. Children are highly sensitive to disturbed feelings in other children. Even small children sense and shy away from deep-seated anxiety or tension in a playmate, if they can't help with it.

Mrs. Ransom described how his friends had been concerned and had tried to cheer him up at first. When they couldn't help, the gradually began to stay away. Each of his parents had tried to help him, had talked to him to try to get behind his sadness, but they had hit a stone wall, and they needed help. They both knew that his depression was being reinforced by their anxiety about him. I set up a time to talk to both of them about him and managed to see him alone on the pretext of an annual checkup.

Matthew was a tall, lean, handsome little boy who had always been friendly, cooperative, and eager to please when I saw him infrequently for his examinations. Now he was noncommittal. As I asked him about himself, he replied in monosyllables and with a kind of hopelessness that led me to comment on it. I asked him whether he knew why he felt so sad and hopeless. He shrugged. I had found nothing physical to account for his mood and I assured him of that. Temporarily, he brightened a bit and said, "I didn't think you would, but my mother hoped there was something you could cure." I said, "Didn't *you?*" He replied with a rather grateful look, "I wish you could make me feel better." "Matt, suppose we got a doctor who understands these things in kids to talk to you. Would you be ready to work with him?" "You mean a psychiatrist? Am I crazy? I have wondered whether I am or not. I feel so sad all the time. I don't really care about anything anymore. Everyone treats me like I'm crazy and maybe I am."

For a child this age to touch on his fears about himself with such awareness was rare in my experience. I assured him that I didn't think he was crazy. I also could promise him that "the doctor who understood such things" could and would help him. I knew this from the way he was appealing to me for help. When a child can reach out so clearly, the first and biggest step toward therapy is already achieved.

We did get Matthew into the hands of an expert child psychiatrist and his therapy has gone smoothly. In our brief interview, he had not only appealed for help by expressing his sadness, but he had demonstrated his readiness to work on it. Matthew was an unusually thoughtful, serious boy who had covered up some of his turmoil for a long time. He had been a too-high achiever as a small child and in the first few years of school. He had been plagued with asthma every time he had a cold or played hard and he would always see this as failure, or badness, in himself. He had begun to fail in his attempts to achieve in school because of a subtle learning disability which surfaced in the second and third grades. He blamed himself for this failure, too. His father and brothers were high-achievers also, and being surrounded by them created more inevitable pressure for this sensitive, caring young boy. These inner and outer pressures, seen as failures by Matthew, piled up to create the symptoms of sadness in him. Sadness could be seen as covering his disappointment in himself. Fortunately, his parents were able to see this and help him. Therapy helped them all to become more aware of these patterns and to deal with them more openly and effectively. Matthew was a different and happy young boy a year later.

Matthew's case offers several clues for parents who are concerned about such a symptom in a child. First of all, his age was most important. At 9, a boy who was as popular and successful as he was should have felt good about himself. Peers are a critical part of one's self-image at this age. The fact that he derived little satisfaction from them, and that their own concerns about him drove them away from him showed how deep-seated Matt's sadness was. His parents' inability to help him, although they had tried, was further evidence of how much he was worried about himself. The duration of his sadness was another signal. The most important factor of all, however, and one which worked toward his successful therapy was his awareness of his need for help. The fact that he could reach out to me when I provided the chance in my office was a real sign of how strong and vital this boy was, in spite of his feelings of inadequacy. Matt's case certainly reinforces the importance of parents and physicians taking a child's own concerns seriously.

GUIDELINES

What are the steps that parents should follow when a child appears sad?

1. Take the child seriously. Trying to jostle or to joke a child out of a sad mood is devaluating to her. Unless she is openly using her sadness to provoke or to gain unnecessary attention, it should be respected as an important sign. Often, by taking it seriously, a parent can help her understand it also.

2. Observe when the sadness occurs. Does it surface at inappropriate times or very often during the day? Does the child stop playing with peers when she is sad? If she responds with sadness after a reprimand or a frustration, it would be easy to see this as appropriate and not necessarily significant. If she responds to every slight frustration with sadness, a parent should begin to see her as more sensitive than she need be, and her feelings listened to carefully. If, and more seriously, sadness invades her joyful experiences as well, it is time to take her symptoms even more seriously.

3. Attempt to get behind the symptom to understand the causes for it. If, by understanding it yourself as a parent, you can uncover a set of obvious and acute reasons, it is likely that you can help her come to an understanding of them herself. If there are subtler and more deep-seated reasons than you as a parent can understand, it is likely that you and she will need an outside evaluation and help.

4. In any event, a child who is sad needs feelings of closeness and of being cared for. Attempt to set up a special time together and encourage a close relationship. As I have mentioned in previous chapters, I always advise parents to set a special time aside for such a child at least once a week. This must not be shared with anyone else but is for her in a one-to-one way. Talking about this time-to-be the rest of the week makes it become a symbol of the closeness that you and she want to reach. It is not likely that the child will be able or will want to unload any deep secrets while the feelings of sadness are strong. It may not even be advisable to press her to let down her defenses to such an extent. But the symbolic value of saying, "I'm here for you and I am trying to understand because I love you" is very powerful.

5. Understand that many feelings which are basic to a child's personality—feelings of loss, of loneliness, of inadequacy, of anger, of depression—all can be expressed as sadness. The parent's job may be to reevaluate the child's daily life in order to try to come to an understanding of what is overpowering. Sadness should be seen as a cry for help, and valued as an opportunity to help the child. Although childhood for most children is not the totally joyful, carefree state that it is claimed to be, it should be a time when the pleasures of learning about oneself and one's world outweigh the stresses. Much of childhood should be joyous.

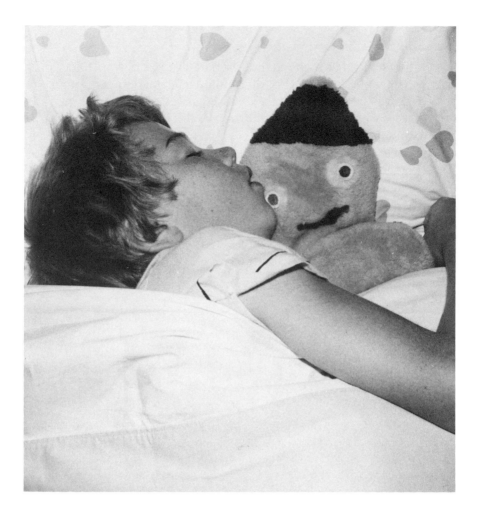

5
THUMBSUCKING AND LOVEYS: STEPS TOWARDS INDEPENDENCE

Our society demands a great deal of independence from a baby, and this pressure starts at birth. In other cultures, mothers or a surrogate are likely to carry the infant around, to sleep with him at night. As soon as he awakens, his periods of activity are met with a feeding, most often at the mother's breast. After he is fed, he is provided the opportunity to look around or to listen to the ever-present caretakers. He is usually carried or swaddled, his body and limbs restrained and inactive. He is never left to cry or to find ways of comforting himself, to find patterns for keeping himself quiet in order to look around or listen. All his needs are met and independence is not expected.

The goals of our society are different. Parents of an infant already are aware that a toddler will have to learn independence to cope with his aggressive peers in a play group. At the age of 3 or 4 he will have to comply with a nursery school teacher (or even a parent) who wants him to climb to the top of a jungle gym or to recite the alphabet. By first grade he will have to find ways of submerging his natural exuberance and his joy in active playing to sit still, along with other 6-year-olds, lined up in quiet rows around a harassed teacher. This is necessary to begin the long process of learning the complex skills required by our society. He *must* be ready, and all parents know it. We may be confused about most of our goals for children, but not in one area—we *know* that we are programming them for a high level of intellectual attainment. In our present society, the ones who aren't ready can become failures by the age of 3 or 4 years.

What a terrible load of responsibility this goal places on young parents! It forces them to search for ways to program their babies with early stimulation, for toys that will press an infant into learning patterns as early as possible. And, in response, the human infant is amazingly capable of compliance. He can be shaped to walk by 9 months, he can recite lists of numbers at age 2, read words by 3, type out sentences by 4. And he can even learn to cope with the pressures that lie behind these expectations. But children in our culture need someone who will cry out, "At what price?"

Infants, children, and even adults have a built-in feedback system that rewards them when they achieve a new task, realize that they have, and say to themselves, "*I* did it!" This feedback, which Piaget calls the "awareness of mastery" and which Robert White called a "sense of competence," spurs an infant on to the next achievement. It provides the awareness of having mastered each step and of being ready to build on it. One can see it in infants at 4 or 5 months as they are pulled up by the arms to stand for the first time. As they come to stand straight on both legs, their faces light up as if to say, "It's me, I'm up!" And at that moment, the goal of standing is set.

When this inner force for learning is coupled with support from the environment, the powerful process of pressures and of rewards which fuels all of learning is set up. Infants respond to these pressures as much as they can, and then are rewarded for each success. Hence, an infant who is learning new, exciting tasks is not in any way a deprived infant. But he may be setting up expensive patterns for himself, and he may need to learn ways of compensating for the inner and external pressures with which he is learning to live.

FINDING CALM AND COMFORT

We need to consider the dependence on a "lovey," or security blanket, or pacifier as ways of compensating. It is difficult to see how an infant or small child can continue to cope successfully with his world unless he learns techniques for self-comfort, for calming himself down, for breaking the driving cycle of activity and exciting mastery into which we are plunging him in our society. Notice how a newborn baby puts his hand to his mouth to quiet himself in order to look around and listen. For older babies and small children, other crutches are necessary. We must see them as an important part of the cycle in which the child builds up to the peaks of excitement we provide and foster, and then brings himself down to a quieter, more self-contained period of rest and recovery.

Take, for example, a newborn infant lying peacefully asleep in his crib. As he begins to awaken, he startles, his arms jerking out in front of him. With the first startle, he rouses a bit, then quiets down again, though to a lighter sleep. After the next startle, he begins to move around in his nest of bedclothes, squirming a bit more actively. As he moves, his eyelids flutter almost imperceptibly and he looks as if he would like to try to open them to look around. Finally, one of his movements causes him to jump in his bed, flinging his arms out and stretching his legs in a reflex startle that we call a Moro reflex. This upsets him and he starts to cry. As he does, he might well set off other startles and more activity, with short cries interspersed. Then, as you watch him, he attempts to gain control over himself. As he builds up to an active state, he makes efforts to turn his head to one side and to set off what we call a tonic neck reflex, similar to a fencing posture. His arm extends, his body arches away from it. As his arm extends, he adjusts it and tends to bring that hand up to his mouth. He makes repeated efforts to bring his fist next to his right cheek. When this is successful and his hand touches his mouth, his movements cease. His eyes widen to look contentedly around. If he is successful in bringing his hand up to his mouth and can latch onto his thumb or finger to suck, he can lie peacefully for long periods, looking around, listening to sounds.

This represents a pattern of self-controlling behavior that is built into the human newborn. He uses it to keep himself quiet in order to learn about the sights and sounds of his new world when he is on his own. We now know that a fetus can bring a hand to his mouth, and we even suspect that this may serve a purpose in the uterus, for it is a definite and established pattern at birth. If the comforting purpose of sucking behavior in the infant is as distinct and as independent of feeding as it seems, it deserves new respect from the adults who are around a baby.

A group of us watched a 5-month-old fetus as he moved about in his mother's abdomen. He was being visualized for us at the Boston Hospital for Women by the new ultrasound technique now in routine use for the intrauterine diagnosis of defects. As he thrashed around, we saw him bring his hand up to his mouth, root around on it, extract one finger, and begin to suck on that tiny finger. I could barely see the finger, but I could see his sucking movements. When he began to suck, he quieted down peacefully, to our utter amazement and his mother's delight. She said, "He's already so active at times that I am really relieved to see that he knows how to quiet himself!" She told us that she had an older, hyperactive child who had had a problem with self-control, and she dreaded another difficult baby. Seeing him able to quiet himself gave her more courage to face this new infant. His fingersucking was already serving a purpose for both of them.

This mother had pointed to one of the most important uses of thumbsucking for a baby, that of maintaining control over himself at difficult times. In the newborn nursery I sometimes see babies who are overly sensitive to the stimuli around them, who react to the slightest noise or movement by a sudden start and go on to cry right away. This hypersensitivity may be a problem later. Overreactivity is likely to lead to a great deal of uncontrollable crying in early infancy. Overreactive babies are tough on their parents, as they can cry inconsolably in the first few months and for long periods. By the end of the third month, when their crying is likely to let up, they begin to resort to rather constant activity as an overreaction to these same events in their environment. As such an infant grows older, he can remain easily distracted and find it difficult to concentrate on a task whenever another new stimulus comes along. We often can predict this in an infant, and recently I have been urging the mother of such a baby to "teach" her infant to suck his thumb. As soon as he can master his own hand-to-mouth behavior, she can help him learn to get hold of his thumb. When he can, his activity will calm down and he will be able to control himself. As long as his thumb is firmly in place, he can begin to pay attention to things around him without flying apart. When he loses his thumb, his activity is likely to begin all over again. Parents with an active, sensitive baby often see their baby's thumbsucking as his most important calming maneuver. A very active, reactive child needs such a way of calming himself more than do most children.

A PARENT'S WORRIES

In our culture, thumbsucking or dependency on a blanket or on a comforting "lovey" like a teddy bear are considered bad habits. Parents whose 1- or 2-year-old depends upon sucking his fingers to calm himself down speak of this as if it were a sign of disturbance: "How can I get rid of his thumbsucking?" or "When can I take her blanket away from her?"

I have asked mothers why they feel they should interfere. Perplexed at such a question, they reply, "It looks as if I weren't a good mother. And suppose he goes on to need his blanket when he goes to school. He'll be the laughingstock of his friends." When I ascertain that the child does not withdraw from events, nor does he hide behind his "habit" to get away from people around him, I can reassure the mother that this habit is not abnormal. Since many disturbed or withdrawn children do hide behind their thumbs to get away from the overwhelming world around them, this association with disturbance has given these habits a bad name. A child who uses his lovey to help him adjust to the world needn't be thought of as being in trouble.

Nearly all children in our culture need a crutch to help them manage. We are pressing ourselves toward ambitious goals and we push our children along with us. Babies and children are marvelously competent. They live up to pressure. They are excited and stimulated by their achievements. They live up to expectations with delight. Competence gathers its own steam and they begin to demand a great deal of themselves. By the end of the first year, their own desire to perform matches their parents'.

The need for such self-comforting patterns as thumbsucking and cuddling a lovey becomes apparent as one observes how small children use them. When they are tired and yet can't let themselves stop, they fall back on a familiar self-comforting pattern of behavior in order to calm themselves down.

As pretty, wide-eyed Sarah played in my office, she literally jumped for joy as she spotted and explored each new toy. She squealed along with a firetruck's noisemaker, she pushed on the pedals of the rocking horse. Although she's seen toys like this before and might have been bored, she wasn't. She made up for her mother's interest in talking to me by generating her own excitement in my playroom. She took toys to her mother and me for approval from time to time, but she also respected her mother's need to be involved with me. She was a charming, exciting little girl to watch as she played. After a while she began to run out of steam, and turned to her thumb. As she sat on the floor, exploring a puzzle with her right hand, she sucked perfunctorily on her left thumb. It was clear that she's used up her resources and we needed to pay attention to her. As we turned to her, out came her thumb and she brightened up. She had revived herself and was ready to go again.

When it was time to examine Sarah, her mother went to pick her up. Sarah measured the situation and lay back on the floor as if to protest. Her mother said, "Sarah, don't! You know the doctor wants to see you. Come sit in my lap." Dutifully, Sarah allowed herself to be picked up, arms and legs hanging limply. As she was undressed in her mother's lap, her face slack, again she inserted her left thumb in her mouth. Each piece of clothing as it came off was observed by Sarah as if she were giving up one more layer of defenses. The thumb remained in place. When the last piece was about to come off, I said, "You can leave on her underpants." Sarah glanced up at me gratefully as if to thank me for this one shred of recognition of her plight. As I came up to kneel at her mother's feet, my stethoscope and instruments in hand, I also brought her dirty, smelly and beloved bunny rabbit. She clutched him (or her?) in her right hand, chomping on her thumb. She allowed me to examine her and her beloved bunny without any protest. At first her thumb remained in her mouth, but gradually it dropped out as she became more interested in the examination. At that point, she engaged me by handing me her bunny to examine. She even smiled at me as I said, "But your bunny doesn't know how to open his mouth. Can you show him?" After a little while her thumb went back in her mouth. This brief but important way of letting herself recover and revive seemed so critical to her that it surprised me when her mother said, "See!" There goes her thumb again! What can I do to stop her?"

Sarah's efficient use of her thumb was not only understandable, it was resourceful, and it suggested competence rather than weakness. When she was overwhelmed by an unfamiliar situation, she could manage it if she were allowed to use this crutch. As she started to suck, her eyes glazed slightly while she pulled herself together. Then she was ready to face whatever confronted her. The crutch became a bridge to the next demanding situation. A remarkable combination of immaturity and competence!

SUCKING: A UNIVERSAL NEED

Since a child's need for such a crutch seemed to stir up feelings of guilt in her parent, I wondered how best to explain its role. Many years ago, in order to try to establish some norms in my own mind,

I studied a group of babies who seemed well adjusted and whose parents obviously loved them. If I could determine that thumbsucking behavior was engaged in by all these healthy babies, I could offer reassurance to worried parents. The babies I studied were not neglected or misused; nor were the parents pushing them in any unusual way. I asked 80 parents to keep a daily record of how much time and under what circumstances the infants fell back on thumb- or fingersucking. I learned a great deal from the study.

First of all, almost all babies had some pattern of falling back on some part of their body, or on a "lovey." The breastfed, contented babies sucked *more* than did the bottlefed ones. I wondered why, and mothers told me: "She seems to enjoy the sucking, and even if I let her suck for nearly an hour, she still will follow this feeding by sucking on her thumb. It's as if she wanted two things—to be able to give up the breast when she's full and still to have the pleasure of sucking. If she sucked on the breast, she got too full. If she used her thumb, she was often more comfortable."

I found that fingersucking started in the newborn period and was reserved for transitions—when going to sleep, waking up, resting during an exciting play session, or giving up a feeding after being satiated. Later on it was used when a toddler got too excited and needed to calm down. It seemed to be a small child's way of adjusting to the many demands of his world.

The frequency and duration of this reliance increased to as much as four hours a day by the age of 7 months (see Figure 1). Then it began to decrease in frequency and intensity. As babies were learning a new skill, such as reaching, sitting up, crawling, or walking, it increased during the frustrated learning period. But when the new step was achieved at last, it began to decrease. After crawling began it decreased steadily through the rest of the first year. I found that very few children used their thumbs by 5 or 6, except in real stress or transition periods. They did not hang onto an "immature" pattern of dependency unless their parents had tried to stop them earlier. When parents had intervened and attempted to interfere with these patterns, their disapproval seemed to reinforce the child's need for his or her security "habit." When it persisted in spite of the parents, it seemed to be because it was a very important crutch for the child. In any event, it seemed to be a mistake to try to deprive a child of it in infancy.

Thumbsucking or fingersucking is a natural and even desirable behavior for the infants at certain points in his day. For example, when

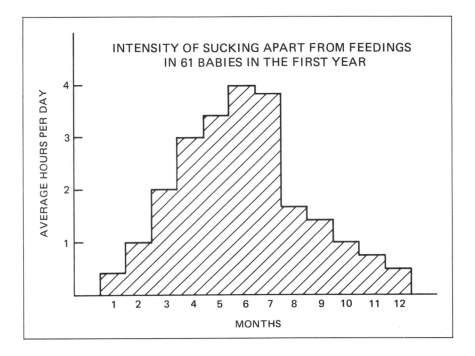

he is tired, bored, or frustrated, the resourceful infant will fall back on a comforting and self-controlling behavior such as sucking his thumb. With this as a crutch, he can pull out of his stimulating, exciting world and reorganize. He can vegetate, recover, and get ready for the next exciting interaction with the world. During a period of frustration over learning a new task or facing a new demand from the world around him, he can recover on his own and get strength to try again. As long as thumbsucking doesn't consume an excessive part of an infant's life, or become a way in which he withdraws from all kinds of pressure, a parent needn't become concerned. I barely can understand why thumbsucking developed such a bad image and led to an era when parents tried to stop it, thus reinforcing it as a habit. Now that parents are no longer as concerned or as interfering, few children use it as a "habit" after 5 or 6 years of age. Even dentists are more relaxed about it and are willing to enter into a more reasonable attitude, taking the position that any damage to mouth structure which is incurred before age 5 can be taken care of later, and maybe the psyche can't be adjusted as easily. As a guideline, I would expect a good deal of fingersucking in the first year, less in the active second year, and still less after the third and fourth year so that he will fall back on it only when he is tired, unhappy, or bored. Such a pattern might persist into the sixth or seventh year. However, if thumbsucking and withdrawal occurs too often and is being used as a shield, it becomes a warning signal of an unhappy child.

PACIFIERS AND LOVEYS

Many parents prefer pacifiers to thumbs. Pacifiers probably serve the same purpose and can be used in much the same way. I am prejudiced in favor of fingersucking because the equipment is all there—the child has it when he wants it. In the first, learning years, a pacifier is likely to be offered at someone else's discretion. It is true that later on a parent can tie the pacifier around the baby's wrist or on a ribbon to his bed so he can find it more easily by himself. This should be done when it already has become the baby's way of comforting himself. But it still leaves him at the mercy of an outside decision maker. So, if all things are equal, I prefer fingers for this important crutch. But things are not always equal, and many active, fussy babies cannot find their fingers to suck. For those babies and their parents a pacifier becomes a godsend—a way the baby can shut out all the disturbing, interfering motor activity that won't allow him to quiet down enough to "make it" with his parents and those around him. But remember that when it has become his crutch, it will not be fair to take it away from him when you decide he has had enough. For, as with fingersucking, he will need his crutch in the second and third years as well as in infancy. To remove it before he can become attached to another "lovey" would be cruel. By the third year, I have found that a child can be "seduced" into accepting a teddy bear or a doll for his lovey. But it must be substituted slowly and at the child's pace, not at the parent's!

I suggest that the pacifier be tied to the new lovey for a period and the child prepared for the eventual substitution. After talking about it, agreeing upon it, and *after* the child is 3, the doll or animal usually can take the place of the beloved pacifier. In any event, beware of an abrupt removal. It is unfair as well as unwise, and may precipitate anxiety the child can't handle. He should be able to count on the pacifier when he needs it and for as long as he needs it.

In order to help him learn how to use it at appropriate times and in an appropriate place, a parent can restrict the pacifier or lovey to his room or his bed after the age of 3. Most children, if promised their "crutch" later, are willing to wait until bedtime or relaxation time. If the child is under particular stress, such as going on a trip, or going to the doctor, he certainly should be allowed to take his pacifier or lovey along.

LOVEYS SHOULD BE CELEBRATED!

To think that a child is resourceful enough and endowed with enough leftover caring to be able to invest it in a doll or a teddy or a blanket makes me feel hopeful about him and his future capacity for loving other people and other things. When I make a house visit, I like to find a dirty, smelly, worn-out animal for which the child has obviously cared repeatedly and long.

When I went to see 3-year-old Mark at his parent's apartment nearby, I found him miserable, clinging to his mother. I suspected that he had an earache. Although we'd made friends in my office at his last checkup, he was not the same easygoing little boy I'd seen then. Whenever I came near him, or when I looked at him, he wailed loudly and burrowed into his mother's lap. I suspected that we'd have a difficult time with his examination unless I could help him with his apprehension.

I looked for and found a very dirty, tattered teddy bear in one corner. It had begun to lose its stuffing and one beady eye had gone. As I picked it up, I saw out of the corner of my eye that Mark was watching me very carefully. He cried out, "No! No!" as if this rather pitiful toy were a part of himself that I was approaching. His mother calmed him and I said, "Mark, may I hold your friend and bring him to you? He feels so sad that you are ill that he'd like to comfort you. Will you hold him?" Mark clutched the animal carefully to him. I knew I'd found the right toy to make a bridge between us. As his mother held him, he held "teddy" for my examination.

I first approached teddy with my stethoscope. Very quietly and briefly I placed it on the toy, then I tried it on Mark's mother's chest. He brushed it away from her. I made several passes at the toy and at his mother before Mark's labored breathing and the anxiety in his eyes began to subside. Finally, with reassuring words, I was able to place the stethoscope on his chest, making him part of a triad. Soon I was able to complete a satisfactory exam of Mark's chest, abdomen, neck, and at last his ears, by using his teddy as a demonstration of what I'd do when I looked at him. Although this exam took a few minutes longer, I was not only able to examine a quiet child, but Mark's trust in me had been captured. When I needed to examine his throat, saved for the last maneuver, I shone my light into teddy's mouth. "Mark, he doesn't know how to open his mouth and how to put out his tongue. Would you show him?" Mark dutifully opened his mouth wide. I asked his mother to show him how to put out his tongue with a wide-open mouth. He watched her to imitate her successfully. We had been through an entire exam without a tear, thanks to his beloved "teddy."

When a child is ill, he can use his lovey to adjust to being miserable and sick. I use it whenever he must be hospitalized and left alone in a strange unwelcoming environment, for I know that a child with a lovey will have an easier time.

Should you foster a lovey? I think you should. But if you decide to, remember that you cannot foster such a relationship when you surround a baby with lots of toys in his crib. Hence, I would urge that you and he come to an agreement early on as to which toy will be his "lovey" when he goes to sleep, when he needs to be alone, when he needs to find his own comfort or companion when there is no other. And if society begins to close in on him and his lovey with its inevitable, senseless disapproval, there are many ways of protecting him and his lovey. If it is a blanket and it is too big and dirty, cut it in half, and wash one half at a time. If it is a teddy bear and it is coming apart, patch it together. If it is filled with straw or hair or kapok and he is allergic to its contents, you can refill it with foam rubber. In other words, I would urge you to respect his love affair and his need for dependence on this extension of himself, for as long as he needs it. By 6 or 7 years of age most children have begun to substitute relationships with other children and toys that are more interesting. But how nice it is to have had a beloved object on which to bestow a part of oneself!

If a thumb or a beloved object can help a child to grow up, it seems obvious to me that we should treasure them. As children mature, other loves and interests will replace these, but the inner sense of competence they will have learned early from such self-reliant patterns will serve them well.

GUIDELINES

Here are a few suggestions that might make it easier for parents to tolerate these "habits" in their children:

1. Plan early for a "lovey" or a crutch that you can tolerate later.

Make it one you don't mind looking at through the first few years, for, once he has attached himself to it, you shouldn't take it away.

2. Don't give your baby a bottle full of milk in bed. We know now that a baby can ruin his future teeth by having milk in his mouth all night. A 6-year-old's permanent teeth will be discolored and full of cavities because he has had a bottle of milk in bed with him in his first few years. If he needs a bottle as a lovey, be sure it's a bottle with water. If not, give him some other kind of "lovey"—a toy or a blanket—or allow him to use his thumb.

3. Babies are likely to become attached to a piece of cloth or a blanket as they go into their cribs for sleep or rest. Give him one that you can wash and cut into small pieces. He will drag around a large blanket, getting it dirty. If you cut it up in smaller pieces, he can love it long enough to be sure it's invaded by all the choice smells he relies on, but part of it can be washed from time to time without having it all lose its familiarity.

4. If as a parent you'd rather he relied on a toy or an acceptable object as he gets older, give it to him as a special lovey from the first. One toy is more important than a bed full of toys. Even though an infant may seem to attach himself to an armful of toys, one will become more meaningful if it is separated out as "the" lovey. A new doll can be great, but you'd better plan on the fact that he will love it when it's ragged and dirty too. The dirtiest, smelliest, most bedraggled toy represents his most beloved object. One should respect the importance of this friend and treat the lovey as an extension of the child.

5. If the need to switch from a bottle to a more "mature" lovey occurs in a small child, find one that the child can have for many years to come. First, begin to talk about it and enhance its meaning for the child. Each night, tie the new toy to the bottle and talk about how "someday" he will take the lovey to bed instead of the bottle. Meanwhile, since they are tied together, he can switch his allegiance to its smells, to the new object in the presence of the old. After his introduction has been made and after it has been discussed at some length, the bottle can be given up in favor of the newer lovey.

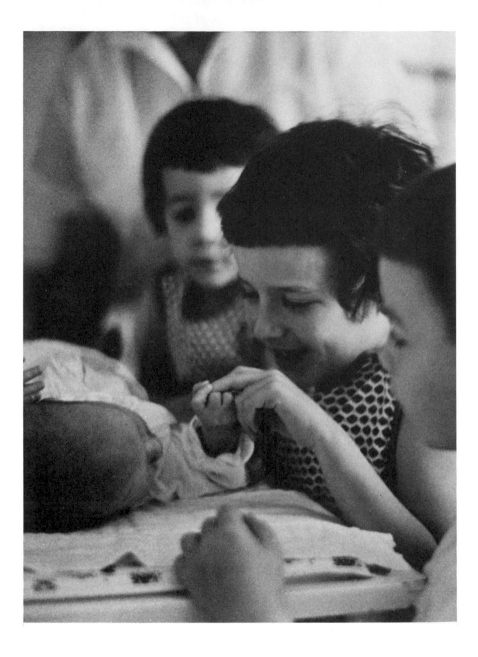

6
SPACING CHILDREN

A long with the blossoming love affair with the first child comes the question, "*Must* I have another child?" After the initial adjustment to the first baby, and when the first few months of colic are over, new parents begin to experience the euphoria of being in love. Every time they look at their 4-month-old, she smiles back at them adoringly. A vocalization from the parent produces a sigh or an "ooh" in response. The baby wriggles all over as she attempts to communicate with the hovering parent. Few moments in life are as delicious as these minutes of reciprocal communication with an alert, vocalizing infant. A parent feels competent and in control of the world.

It is hard, however, to be head over heels in love without the nagging fear that sooner or later it must come to an end. In our calvinist society, we are steeped in the foreknowledge that sooner or later we must pay for our blessings. The anguish with which parents face this question of giving up the love affair with their first child in order to share it with a second is surprisingly painful. With the increasing pressure on parents to limit their families, there is a parallel feeling that an only child may be "spoiled" or may "suffer." These days parents feel that one child will be too lonely if both of them are working. They feel they should have a second child in order to give the first a friend and a close relative. So, many families today tend to think of a family of two children as their goal. Women who interrupt careers to have their families feel they should have the second child soon so they can "get on back to work." Another unconscious reason that dominates parents' thinking is more subtle. Since the first baby has created a triangle, and each parent wants the baby, they tend to think that two babies would give each of them a baby of his or her own. So the idea of having two together to complete the family is a common one. The fact that this comes up in the midst of the joyous first year with the first child is no coincidence.

ENDING THE HONEYMOON

In my office, I find I can expect a question about when to space children at certain times during the first child's development. These times are related to the first child's spurts of independence. The young mother of a 5-month-old baby will ask, "Now that Jean is growing up, when should I start another baby?" The reluctance to give up Jean is couched in the word "should," as if it were some sort of penance for caring so deliciously about Jean. The timing of this question seems incongruous if one looks at Jean. She is a round, soft mass of creases and dimples. As she lies on the examining table, she looks carefully around the room, her face serious as she surveys each new object. Every minute or so, she glances back at her mother or father leaning on the table near her, talking to me. As she looks at one of them, they look back reassuringly. Her face crinkles, her eyes soften, and she smiles gratefully up at them, her legs and arms wriggling a bit as she thanks them with her whole body. This lasts only a few seconds. She returns to her job of processing the information about the strange place. They return to their job of communicating with me. But in that moment I have witnessed an example of the depth of their attachment to each other. Each of them has felt a surge of loving feeling, and each has felt deeply the importance of the other's presence. The baby has said with her eyes, "You are my anchor, and I can afford to be here in such a strange, exciting new place because I can look back at you and you'll be there!" The parents have had a chance to feel the depth of their own importance to this new individual.

Doesn't it seem amazing that, at that point, one of the parents asks, "What do you think about having another baby?" Or that Jean's breastfeeding mother will ask, "When should I wean her?" If I pursue either of these questions with them, it will become apparent that they don't want another baby yet, nor does her mother want to wean her.

But these questions guard against caring too much and help to balance the burgeoning attachment. And Jean has begun to dilute it herself. She interrupts a feeding again and again to look around, to listen to a door close in the next room, to gurgle up at her mother, to smile brightly across the room at her father. To her mother, these are signals that Jean doesn't need her as much any more. For Jean, they represent a burst in her cognitive development, a rush of new interest in and awareness of the world around her. In some way they represent the beginning of independence. For her parents, they seem to be a re-minder of the future when Jean will indeed become independent of them.

It is important to recognize all these feelings before planning another baby. A mother in particular finds it very difficult to contem-plate the separation from the first baby. I have seen mothers break down in my office as they told me about being pregnant a second time. The prospect of "deserting" the first for the second looms large, and it can be depressing to have to face the prospect of diluting the intensity of this relationship. Hence, I would urge parents to save the first year for the first baby so that it can be entirely hers and entirely enjoyed. Even sharing it with a fetus can infringe on the pure joy of that relationship.

CLOSELY SPACED BABIES

Breast-feeding mothers run a particular risk of inadvertently conceiv-ing the next pregnancy. I have seen many instances of unexpected second pregnancies which were started in this period, the mother thinking she was protected by lactation and unable to predict when she was ovulating because her periods had not returned. If she is not careful, she may start the second baby before she is ready to give up the first one. Having two children as close as 10 – 18 months is comparable to having unequal twins, and they are even called "Irish twins." Raising them sucessfully certainly can be done, and it can even be fun at times, but it is hard work while they are little. Having two dependent individuals of different ages is demanding both physically and emotionally. The danger for the babies is that a physically ex-hausted mother is likely to lump them together. Her tendency will be either to treat them as if they were babies who were the same age or to press the slightly older toddler to grow up too quickly. As the toddler resists by acting just like the baby, a mother unconsciously resents the demands on her and presses the older one to take more responsibility than she is ready for. When they finally get older and less demanding, it is easier to sort them out as individuals. And in the end they may be closer to each other because they are so close in age.

Given a choice in planning a family, parents should plan with regard to their own energies and tolerance. Their own reasons for hurrying or delaying in spacing children may be the best guidelines they can follow. A mother who wants to have her family quickly so that she can get back into the marketplace may resent being kept at home for too many years and may indirectly take it out on her family. A father who feels he needs time between each child to save up for their future may be saying that he can assimilate one child and one responsibility at a time. The problem for most families is that they can't anticipate and plan in advance to accommodate their levels of energy and strength.

WAITING FOR INDEPENDENCE

If you can feel that you've really belonged completely to your first child and she is solidly on her way to independence, it becomes easier to share her with the next baby. The independence of the child's second year makes it easier to think about giving attention to a new baby. Inevitably the new baby will demand time and emotional energy. Almost as inevitably, a mother will push the older child to grow up quickly when the new baby arrives. In third-world cultures, there is usually a ritual associated with weaning the older child when the mother is expecting a new baby. She openly will push the responsibility for the older child onto another member of the family—the grandmother, an aunt, or an older sibling. She will repeat again and again in a ritual manner. "Now I must turn my back on you so that I can devote myself to the new one." Although this is often done in a harsh way, I have seen the anguish that the mother hides as she gives up her child. But she knows she must force herself to "turn her back" or she won't have the energy available to nurture a new baby.

As the toddler hits the independence of the second year, she needs time to sort out her choices. Does she really want to be independent? Does she mean "no" when she says it so forcefully, or did she really mean "yes?" After a flaming temper tantrum that leaves her exhausted, she needs a parent to help her sort out the reason for the tantrum, to help her learn limits on herself. Who else can refuel her to go on searching for the boundaries and the strengths which will help her to become an independent person? If a mother cannot be available at this time and cannot see this struggle for independence as being both critical and exciting, both she and the baby will feel frustrated throughout the second year. If the mother is too exhausted by a second baby, she may lose her sense of humor and perspective on this rich period of learning and testing. Ideally, then, a mother might plan the second child to arrive after some of this second-year turmoil has had a chance to be resolved.

Parents who wait for two to three years between their children may wonder whether the children will be too far apart to be friends as they get older. Will they be able to depend upon each other? My own experience has led me to the feeling that if the parents can enjoy the spacing of the children, the children will be better friends for it. If parents are stressed by children who are too close in age, the children will spend most of their childhood in sibling rivalry. Sibling rivalry is always aimed at parents. Children are inevitably rivalrous, and when parents do not get involved, they will sort out their competitive feelings by themselves. If the children's rivalry makes parents feel they have not been adequate parents to each child, *then* the feelings of rivalry are reinforced and may outweigh the more positive feelings between siblings. This is another reason for planning children around the parents' requirement for available energy. Two- to three-year spacing often fits into such needs. By the age of 2 or 3 most toddlers are basically independent. Their mobility is established, their play is rich and can be independent, they should have established independent eating and sleeping habits, and many of them are on their way to understanding the advantages of being toilet trained.

In addition, by 2 years of age children are ready for group play with others their own age. A peer group can be the highlight of a toddler's week. The learning that occurs as they play with each other, the discharge of tensions and the sorting out of negativism that can take place in a small play group demonstrates the marvelous availability of children of this age to each other. This means that a mother can set up regular play groups with other mothers, or she can feel comfortable about placing her toddler in a day or group setting—*for her own sake*—so that she can be available to her new infant. Spacing children two or three years apart can be made easy and productive for everyone in the family.

THE NURTURING EXPERIENCE

Parents who choose to space children more than three years apart can find many benefits. By the age of 4 or 5, a child is really ready to participate in the care of a new baby. She can feel the baby belongs to her. She can learn to feed, to hold, to rock, to diaper, to comfort, and to play with the new baby. Once she recovers from the initial disappointment that the new baby isn't her own age and her equal in the games she's planned, she can begin to participate with her parents in the game of learning about the new baby and watching the baby achieve each new developmental step. The other day, 5-year-old Leslie came bursting into my office saying, "Dr. B., you should see my baby walking! He don't fall down any more!" With that, he rushed over to his 11-month-old brother and held out his hands to his brother. His brother grinned all over at this attention from his hero. He gratefully and greedily grasped Leslie's hands to pull up to stand. Barely balancing, he held tightly to his brother's outstretched arms to teeter across the room. As Leslie backed up to lead his brother on, he chortled with delight, "See! See! Isn't he great?" As I watched this elegant example of an older child not only teaching the baby to walk but also passing on to him the excitement of learning, I thought to myself, "Isn't a younger child fortunate to have such an opportunity for learning about the thrill of living?" Leslie and his brother are not only acquiring learning skills from each other, they also are learning what it means to be deeply dependent upon each other.

At 4 or 5, a child is naturally ready to care for and teach a smaller individual. Margaret Mead pointed out to me that one of the most serious deprivations in our culture is that children in this 4–7-year-old age group so rarely have the opportunity to care for smaller children. She pointed out that in most cultures around the world, older siblings are expected to be responsible for younger children. Thereby, they learn the ingredients of nurturing and prepare to be parents when their time comes. A space of several years between children automatically provides this kind of experience for the older child. And for the younger child, the opportunity to learn from an older sibling is a real privilege. Our last child acquired most of his skills and has learned most of his values from the careful, patient teaching of his older sisters. His hunger to learn from them was founded on a kind of blind adoration, which is different from a baby's feelings when parents try to teach the same tasks. I always have been struck with the eager, longing expression with which a baby or toddler watches an older child. And I am amazed at the imitative learning that takes place when an older sibling stops briefly to teach a small child a new skill.

LEARNING TO SHARE

Learning to share may be the most difficult aspect of growing up in a family. But it is also the most important thing one can learn in childhood, for learning to share means learning to understand the other person's feelings. Whenever I have a toddler who is a hair-puller or a biter, I urge her parents to find her another hair-pulling or biting toddler and then to leave them together. One will attack the other; the one who gets attacked will look absolutely shocked and show that she is suddenly realizing that it hurts to be bitten or to have one's hair pulled. She will never do it again. This can be the first vivid lesson in what it means to act upon another person. Learning to share can be painful but rewarding.

Parents have their own problem with sharing. In thinking about a new baby, few parents feel really competent to care for more than one child. And this sense of inadequacy may well convey itself to the first child as a fear of not being available to her. Having more than one child does demand that parents plan to divide their attention. Saving a special time for the older child becomes as important as being available to the baby.

When you are expecting a new baby, prepare the older child for the separation and then for the changes in your relationship. Let her learn to participate with you and identify with you as a caregiver for the new baby. Instead of pushing her away "to protect the new baby," let her learn how to be tender and gentle, how to hold and to rock, how to feed the new baby. She will feel it's her baby, too.

After the new baby is at home, and many things are demanding your time and energy, be sure you save a special time for the older child or children *alone* and without the new baby nearby. Each older child deserves a small segment of protected time from each parent. The amount of time doesn't matter, but the quality of it does. One hour a week for each child with each parent can be like pure gold in maintaining your relationships. It must be protected for that child *alone* and should be hers to use in any way she pleases. And it should be talked about all the rest of the week: "Even though I don't have time, we *will* have our time together later. And it's my time with you (and without the baby) because you are my first baby, and I still care about you." Or from Daddy, "I wish I could stay home from work with you, but you know I can't. But we will have a time—our time—later this week, when you and I can do *our* things together. That's because you are my girl (or boy), and I wish all week I could be with you." Special times may be short, but their quality cements a family.

When one is planning a large family, spacing can become even more important. There is no question in my mind that older children are of enormous value to the smaller ones. A third or fourth child is almost inevitably better off for having the cushioning of parental experience and for having the older ones to learn from and rely upon. A large family is rarer and rarer these days, for good reason, but the children in small families are likely to be losing something. Older children in a large family have the chance to nurture and to watch the parents nurture their small brothers and sisters. Numerous studies show that parenting one's own child is significantly easier for parents who have participated in large families and who have shared the experience of raising smaller siblings. Mothers who have seen their own mothers breastfeed a new baby in the family are almost universally successful in breastfeeding their own babies. But having too many small, demanding children can be a nightmare. Spacing children at least two years, but preferably three to five years, may make a large family more fun.

What about mothers who are over 35 and feel their time for childbearing is limited? Should they rush to have children as close together as possible? I would certainly say "no." An older mother will find each baby demanding, exhausting, and uniquely pleasurable. It is probably even more important as an older parent to enjoy each baby to the fullest, for the physical labor needs to be balanced by rewards.

Spacing of children should be a selfish decision, with as much consideration for one's own available energies and needs as possible.

GUIDELINES

1. Do not allow your own problems with separation from the older child to keep you from sensing the child's loneliness.
2. Prepare the older child for the separation of your going away to have a new baby. Timing may be important—too early may be frustrating, but it is important to have it out in the open and talked about by the time you need to leave.
3. Bring a special "lovey" home for the older child to play with and to imitate you as you care for your baby.

4. Set up special occasions for the older child to hold and care for the new baby.
5. Save special times to be with the older child and plan them without the new baby.
6. Talk about these special times at all other times to make them symbolize how much you miss the earlier one-to-one relationship.
7. When parents are not too stressed by sibling rivalry, it is easier for the child to express her feelings.
8. Be prepared for the developmental regressions that are likely to occur in the older child, for example, increased negativism and temper tantrums, a recurrence of wetting the bed, baby talk, wanting to be treated like a baby, etc. The older child usually will regress in the areas she has just mastered, but the regression may be less obvious and less specific. A parent's role is to support, not to punish or to show disappointment. If this regression lasts too long, the parent can begin to explain it to the child as a sign of how much she is identifying with the new baby. Giving her an understanding of herself can be therapeutic.
9. Special attention to the older child's needs for other outlets will certainly pay off. In the second and third years, a toddler can work out many of her problems at home in a play group with her peers. The natural negativism of the second year can find outlets in imitative play with other negative 2-year-olds.
10. All of these point to the importance of deciding when to have a second child on the basis of the parents' ability to have emotional and physical energy left over for the other child. If they are happy in the spacing, the older child will adjust to any configuration.

PART
TWO

COMMON ISSUES

7
DISCIPLINE

The job of disciplining a small child is one of the most difficult, but also one of the most important responsibilities of parenthood. In the 1950s, an era of permissiveness, parents tried to be free of it. They rationalized by saying that each child should explore his own individuality and should find his own limits. By eliminating limits, parents thought they were freeing the child to explore himself and his world freely. When this caused problems, they blamed Dr. Spock. But he was only the scapegoat, for he never recommended such permissiveness.

I remember the dread of being invited out to dinner in the 1950s. One braced oneself to spend the evening with one's friend's children. As the evening wore on, weary, wild-eyed children would climb over the visiting adults, the furniture, the dinner table. As if begging for someone to say "Stop! Go to bed." they would lie down in the middle of the room, crying in a temper tantrum. It was terrible to sit by and see them fall apart. One felt an urge to stop them, to say "No," and to act in a disciplinary way. As they virtually begged to be stopped, their parents became more and more conflicted. "Should we or shouldn't we say no to them?" "Should we or shouldn't we put them to bed? It seems so selfish to ask them to leave the company just because we want them to go." This conflict on parents' part certainly didn't pay off for the children, for they became more and more upset.

They tried harder and harder to communicate their need for parental control.

Since then we have learned that many of these children of the 1950s felt "on their own" when they were small. I have had many of them say to me in my office that they longed for parental firmness, rather than what they felt they received—parental disapproval, unspoken and tense. I am sure their parents would not have admitted to such feelings, but I am sure the children are right. No one could sit by and watch a child tease for discipline without having a reaction of disapproval. Such children were labelled "spoiled" or "anxious" by everyone around them, and their undisciplined behavior in school let them in for teacher and peer disapproval. This behavior was not recognized for what it represented—an anxious search for limits. A spoiled child is an anxious child—searching for relief from his own decision making.

THE CHILD'S SEARCH FOR LIMITS

Since the 1950s, and as these very same children have become parents, there has been a merciful swing away from this kind of permissiveness. It has been recognized for what it was—an abdication of parental responsibility rather than the child-oriented approach it was labelled. We have begun to recognize that small children search for limits on their behavior. When they begin to sense that they are getting out of control, or when they do not know how to stop themselves, they begin to tease or provoke the adults around them. By learning from adults what is acceptable and what isn't, by learning from an understanding, but firm adult how to gain control over a disintegrating ego, a child can begin to learn how to impose limits on himself. Discipline, then, is a parent's role. It may be painful because it is often needed at a time when the parent senses the child's anxiety. But the relief which a small child demonstrates as he settles down after his own vigorous protest, assures the parents that they are on the right track.

Emily is a brown-eyed, brown-haired, rather plump little girl of 2. She had been an easy baby, and her parents were lulled by the first year of blissful communication. When they smiled, Emily smiled. When Emily chortled, they chortled. Emily was charming and they were charmed. Emily had another asset—she was eager to please them. So they basked in mutual admiration and the blissful love affair of the first year. Parenting seemed so easy to her parents that they were already planning a second baby when Emily's second year and her negativism hit. She became just as forceful in her negative responses and in her tempers as she had been in her attempts to please. She became unpredictable to her mother who had been revelling in her predictability throughout the first year. Whereas she had seemed so easy in the first year, Emily changed into a stubborn, determined little girl. If she was thwarted, she lay down to scream. When her mother tried to get her to eat, she threw her food off the highchair. When her mother tried to put her to sleep, she found one excuse after the other to resist or to postpone bedtime. Her parents were shocked and overwhelmed. Mrs. Abt asked me what she had done wrong to create such a monster out of her wonderful Emily. She felt she could no longer take Emily out for fear of the tantrums she seemed to save up for a public place.

The Abts were overwhelmed by this sudden change in Emily's behavior, and they felt angry both at her and with themselves. They felt responsible for her behavior but unable to control it. As a result, they spent most of the day avoiding a confrontation. Their requests to Emily were tentative: Did she want to go to bed? Would she sit down in her highchair? After a few of these tentative requests, she always seemed to have an upset. When they came to me, they were desperate. Emily seemed to be in charge of the household. She was dominating their lives. She woke them in the morning, and kept them up at night. She was not eating at mealtimes, but wanted tidbits from one meal to the next. She never liked whatever she was offered, but led them from one part of the kitchen to another, looking for "something she wanted." She cried so much when they wanted to go out at night that they never dared leave her. Her father literally dreaded coming back to the house at night. Emily's mother had planned to get a job and to leave Emily in a play group but this was no longer even mentioned.

I watched them in my office as we talked. Emily was not the cheerful-looking baby she had been. She was strained and rather driven in her activity. As each parent tried to talk to me, she watched intently. Like those of an observer at a tennis match, her eyes darted from one speaker to the other. She tried to divert them from their concerned pleas to me, with teasing provocative behavior. She climbed up into one lap then the other in her effort to divert her parents' attention. She talked in her new words at an increasing pitch, as if she were competing with them. She put her hands over their mouths; she brought them one toy after another, piling their laps high.

When her parents refused to stop talking to me to acknowledge her, she began to get more and more provocative. She pulled books out of my bookcase, which made them both jump to replace them. She climbed on my desk to insert herself between us as we talked. She began to pull papers off my desk. Meanwhile the toys that were laid out for her were ignored. Obviously, her entire interest was devoted to her mother and father. As she grew more and more excited with her teasing behavior, her eyes became glassy, her face even more strained. Her movements became tense and she even fell rather clumsily into the furniture in the office. She hardly noticed when she fell.

After one rather desperate plea for their attention, she fell onto the floor to wail, rolling back and forth as she did. Her parents looked as disturbed and helpless as she. They asked, "What do we do now? She seems more like a wild little animal than like our Emily."

I looked at the three of them—all miserable, all of them tense and isolated from each other, all feeling deserted and angry. I asked, "Couldn't you pick her up, hold her—just to say you love her?" Her mother started to reach for her, but Emily's wails increased. Her father fairly shouted, "Leave her alone!" He turned to me to say, "She will just be worse. She will kick us and hurt us if we try to help. She is out of control," and then he added sadly, "So are we."

By now, Emily was beginning to stop her wails and was curling up in a little ball, her thumb in her mouth, her other hand pulling on her hair. She looked exhausted.

When I thought about how they had ever gotten to such a situation, the dynamics seemed clear to me. As she had come into the negative second year, and had needed them to adjust with her to a new level of her development, they had been unable to see that her negativism, her demands showed a real need for limit-setting. Either they had been surprised and overwhelmed by this "new" Emily, or they had been unable and unwilling to see what she needed from them. As she searched for limits unsuccessfully, she had become more and more anxious and provocative. This had driven them away and isolated her. She sensed anger and felt as though they were withdrawing from her. She teased even harder to reach them and built up to higher peaks of activity and anxiety. They felt helpless, no longer capable of relating to her or her needs, as their hidden anger immobilized them.

We talked about Emily's need for a more direct approach. Couldn't they tell when she was making a bid for some recognition from them? I was able to point out how anxious she had been as they talked about her, and how desperately she had tried to reach them before she fell apart.

Mrs. Abt began to weep softly as she said, "You know when Emily gets so demanding, I get a reaction that probably comes from my own childhood. No one ever said "No" to me and I grew up frightened of anyone's disapproval. If my parents even looked angry, I fell apart. I ran to my room to hide. I was so fearful that I might displease all the adults around me that I've spent most of my life trying to please people. Emily was like that in her first year. Now that she has changed, she is like someone I cannot understand. It frightens me because I feel as if I just cannot face all of those old feelings from way back. Can't she see that I am helpless when she is like that?" And then she added, "You know until now I did not realize that I was asking this 2-year-old child to take care of me!"

Emily's father confirmed her outburst with his own by stating his own problem with her provocative, negative behavior. "My father was such an autocrat that I swore I would never discipline my child. I felt that anything would be better than the discipline we grew up with. I try to avoid situations with Emily that I know will lead to these breakups but she seems to be smarter than I am. We always get back to one where I *know* I should act. I feel that if I do, I might overreact and hit her or hurt her. It is easier to just turn my back and walk away, or to act as if it were not happening."

By now, both parents had revealed themselves in a self-searching way and they knew as well as I did that their behavior had been dominated by their own needs, and had effectively ignored Emily's. Her father gathered her up to hug and love her. Emily nestled contentedly in his lap. Mrs. Abt said, "Have we ruined her? I am so frightened of her growing up to be a headstrong, spoiled child."

At this point, we were able to talk about Emily's needs—her need for contact with them and with their feelings, even their anger when she was negative and provocative. We talked about her need for limit setting and for discipline before she became as disintegrated as she had been in my office. We could talk about how an honest approach from them to her negative behavior would be reassuring, how limits for her provocative behavior would be felt by her as love from them. She was searching for these limits, which make her feel loved and in contact with them. They were far more desirable to her than the isolation and anger her acting out created. Once they could see their role in setting these limits, they would probably see the return of "their old Emily"—a delightful, reassured little girl.

CHANGING GOALS FOR PARENTS

I was interested in a recent survey by *Redbook* magazine which polled 20,000 young parent-readers around the country for their ideas about discipline. The responses to this survey were enlightening—and enlightened. These young mothers seemed to have a very good idea of why discipline was important—and they all seemed to agree with the fact that it was. Their answers reflected a deep concern that children learn self-discipline by learning about it from their families. No one who responded seemed to have any indecision about the fact that there were times when action was critical. That they felt it could be coupled with reason, with affection, and understanding means to me that they do indeed see it as an important part of the role of parenting. The other side of the coin of love and affection is the setting of limits, and these mothers saw themselves as doing this job in an affectionate, understanding way. Their attitude toward good behavior carries out the same theme—that of rewarding the child in a way that helps *him* understand himself. The goals they saw as uppermost for their children were: honesty, respect for the feelings and property of others, love for home and family, generosity, courtesy, and an ability to get along with others—all of them coupled with self-reliance. These parents saw how an understanding of himself should help a child develop these traits.

The problem with a questionnaire is that the sample of those who respond is likely to be a biased one, in the direction of women who are articulate and already clear about their goals. In addition, responses are liable to reflect the actions that parents wish for and are not necessarily a true reflection of their actions under stress. The wide spread in this survey was reassuring, as were the responses that admitted to childrens' behavior which they did not find acceptable. I found these anecdotes informative, honest reflections of what thoughtful young women were trying to do in guiding their children toward certain goals.

I was particularly interested in the universality of altruism as a major goal. I remember a similar questionnaire which was asked of mothers some 25 years ago. Their top priorities did not include honesty, generosity and respect for others, but were more in the area of achievement—both educational and financial. As I remember, 95% of the mothers were most interested in high academic achievement as a primary goal. I was horrified then, and have remembered it as I watched that generation in the late sixties and early seventies demonstrating against the bigotry and class-locked standards of our generation. The sit-in strikes in universities seemed to me a protest against the stated goals of their parents, and against the omissions which the goals represented: the omission of altruism and of caring for others.

This generation of mothers—if the questionnaire represents them—sees their parental role more as fitting their children to live with others, to develop a kind of self-esteem which will endow them for whatever uncertain future they must face.

GUIDELINES

What are some of the times when discipline is needed and what do you as a parent need to know to decide when to act? The most obvious times necessary for discipline occur in the second year and soon thereafter. By that time, a toddler is getting into all sorts of new, exciting situations. He is mobile and "on his own" most of the day. Driven by the excitement of learning, he gets himself caught in more than he can handle. As he builds up to more and more excitement, his eyes dilate, his hands tremble and explore indiscriminately, his legs keep him going from one place to another. Unable to stop long enough either to take in what he's playing with, or to let himself recover a bit from the high-pitched state of excitement he's in, he begins to fall apart. From his high of exploration, he will inevitably hit bottom. A parent can see it coming, but can't always prevent it. At this point, a temper tantrum or a crying fit can be precipitated by nothing at all, or even by an inadvertent remark from an adult or another child.

Often, the disintegrating toddler will precipitate the crisis himself, to provoke a real response from the adult. For example, one of ours always went for the television set when she wanted to attract our attention. Knowing we didn't want her to play with it, she turned around to be sure we were watching, before she'd go too far. Then with a cry of glee, she'd spring for it—in such a way we knew we had to say "No" to her. Her very teasing peaked to let us know it was now or never. When we did respond with a "No," she tried to size up how to interpret it. "Did we really mean it or could she go on a bit farther?" was obviously passing through her mind. If she felt she could get away with it, she'd take a few more steps, watching us seriously now, to test how much farther she could go. When we would finally say, "Now, that's enough. Stop teasing!" she'd lie down on the floor to cry her heart out. *Of course* we wondered whether we hadn't been far too cruel over such an insignificant thing. *Of course* we felt as though we were taking advantage of her small size and of her inexperience. *Of course* these were the feelings which had incapacitated us in the first place. The amazing thing was to see how she knew she made us feel and directed her screams at us. If we said, "We're sorry, don't feel so badly," her screams would increase, and her legs would pound on the floor. At the point where one of us finally said, "Okay. It's your tantrum. You deal with it. You know you can't play with certain things, and every time you do, I shall stop you," she would stop crying as if by magic. Looking us each right in the eye, with relief on her face, she'd come over to one of our laps, climb up to be cuddled. If one of us could say at that point, "You *know* you can't do that. So you just teased to get me to say 'No' didn't you?" she would look up beatifically, as if we'd certainly misjudged her, but she'd forgive us. The truth was that we'd done the right thing. It settled her turmoil and she was grateful for it. Her "high" was ended and she'd learned that she herself could end it. Over time, these episodes became less expensive to all concerned.

The temper tantrums and the testing episodes of the second and third years demand firmness, coupled with an understanding explanation to the child after the episode is over. In that way, a parent can help a toddler learn to contain himself, and to learn from the discipline.

What about the danger of being overly punitive or of hurting the child physically? A child this age and older can keep on pushing too far, teasing until you lose control. At the end of the day, when parents are tired and ready for a cozy visit with each another, a child may begin to press the hardest for repeated episodes of discipline. The parents need nurturing, too, and may feel pretty angry about being teased. As the teasing builds up, one of them may feel like spanking or slapping the child. If that doesn't work, the tension can build up, until the parent really feels like hurting the child. These are frightening feelings to have. Can one break into the cycle before it goes this far?

One approach is to pick up the disintegrating baby, hold onto him firmly, sit down and rock him calmly and soothingly. As you rock, talk to the child about how upset you both are, and how you both can calm down to have a nice time together. If this reaches the child, it may well break through the upset and you can continue on each others' wavelength. If it doesn't work, and the teasing continues, it may be best to use isolation as a way of setting things. If you are determined that the provocative behavior must stop, a child usually knows it and falls in with your firmness. If he doesn't, putting him in his room "to cool off" gives you both a chance to collect yourselves. Then, a peiod of reconciliation, followed by a short discussion of why it was necessary, and a rewarding time doing something fun together can really help start a better pattern. Each of you will learn from that kind of experience.

The best way to prevent such late-in-the-day buildups is to set up a routine of play or of sharing pleasant experiences before a crisis builds up at the end of the day. Mothers who have been at home all day are often too fed up to think of it, and working parents are too tired to want to give any more. But if a parent can change the atmosphere to a positive one before a crisis begins, or can settle down to share a cozy experience before the child becomes too provocative, the end of the day can be more rewarding for everyone.

Another time at which one can expect breakdowns is when excitement builds up—with the visit of grandparents, or during a visit to a crowded shopping center. Obviously, prevention of a blowup would be infinitely preferable to having to deal with it after it happens. Many mothers find they cannot go shopping with a toddler or a 3-year-old. They know it will end with a screaming breakdown.

Can such situations be prevented? Talking to a child beforehand and preparing for an alternate outcome may help. "If you begin to get too tired, we'll leave, but please don't cry or whine there. People do not like to hear you cry, and they do like you when you are happy." Preparation can be amazingly helpful. But it does not always work, and at those times a firm removal of the child is the only recourse.

How can a parent know when he or she is being too strict all the time? All of us have high standards, and they may be too high. We may expect too much of our children without knowing it, just as we expect too much of ourselves. In our zeal to teach our children to respect others and fit into a demanding society, we may ignore the fact that a child does need to test himself and his world. He may need opportunities for going too far and for finding out what the consequences are. Holding him in all the time may not be as productive as having an occasional blowup. I worry when a child is too good and too eager to please. By the end of the first year, he should be teasing and exploring. He shouldn't be too easily diverted or too easily shut up. An 8-month-old should begin to refuse food. By 10 months he should begin to crawl away from his parents, and by a year he should be teasing in many ways—dropping food off his tray, or his spoon over the side of the table to see whether you will pick it up. If a child is too sensitive to mild criticism, or is too easily dominated, maybe you'd better let up, and reevaluate the atmosphere.

Another warning sign may be loss of a sense of humor, and constant irritability. If a child is under too much pressure, he may become too serious or too anxious. Symptoms of anxiety may show up in any area—feeding, sleeping, toileting, etc. (see Introduction and Chapters 8, 9, and 13). If there are no other reasons why such symptoms and/or a regression into passivity or irritability are happening, it is time to reevaluate what you are doing and whether life is as rewarding as it might be for your child. A thoughtful mixture of fun and of discipline can provide a sense of security and joy for a child— both in himself and in his environment.

8
FEEDING: PLEASURE OR BATTLEGROUND?

For most of the world, feeding children is a matter of life and death. In East Africa, a man provides the land to be worked, but it is a women's job to work it—for it is she who must provide the food for her children. In the third-world societies I have seen, it is a woman's responsibility to be sure that her children are fed. Men may participate in tending and harvesting crops, or hunting and gathering food, but it is a woman's job to prepare and serve it. The culture, through the extended family, provides rituals and taboos about food which show a mother what is necessary and important. She learns all this in childhood as she watches the women in her family gather, prepare, and serve food. When it is her turn with her own family, she has little left to learn—her job is well defined and clear cut. Breastfeeding is the norm, and success with each infant is expected. In such cultures a woman is judged by her ability to raise healthy children.

THE GOOD PROVIDER

Starting in pregnancy, a mother's role as source of nourishment shment is vital. A fetus' development is dependent upon appropriate and adequate intrauterine nutrition. In countries where undernutrition in pregnant women is likely to be close to a starvation level, brain development as well as that of other organs is affected by maternal undernutrition. All the cells in the body are likely to be affected by undernutrition and do not multiply at the same rate as they would if she were decently fed. As much as 40% of the body's cellular growth can be affected if the mother's undernutrition is severe. The brain of the fetus is spared until last and the linear growth of the baby is affected first. For instance, babies we studied in Eastern Guatemala, whose hardworking mothers were on inadequate diets of 1500 calories/day (in this country 2200 calories a day for a resting mother has been estimated as minimal), were all born short and small. Some who were affected the most were also behaviorally inadequate. This seemed to indicate that their brains were underdeveloped, too. They were quiet, difficult to rouse to get social responses, and they slept a lot; their deprived, starving mothers fed them on demand. Demand in these drowsy infants turned out to be three times a day in the neonatal period—at a time when at least six feedings are necessary for proper growth. These babies, at birth, were already doomed to short stature, inadequate brain functioning, low energy, and failure in future development. This is one way in which poverty reproduces itself from one generation to another.

In these deprived cultures, where food is at a minimum and children are affected by nutritional deficiency diseases, rituals are set up which protect a mother from her feelings of guilt. Otherwise, her feelings about what might happen to each child would be too overwhelming; her own survival and that of her other children would be threatened. If a baby ends up with a starvation disease when a mother weans him in the second year, certain rituals and beliefs protect her from feeling responsible. Attitudes toward *kwashiorkor* are a vivid example. Kwashiorkor is a disease of the second year, usually associated with weaning from vital breast milk, and with inadequate food intake. In most cultures where kwashiorkor is a threat, the mother has already turned away psychologically, and become attached to the next baby. The older child is often called "bad" or "no good" for having this deficiency—and no one blames the mother or allows her to blame herself. It is said to be the child's responsibility by then. So strong is the denial about this deficiency disease that it was poorly understood until late in the century. Now we do understand that it is a combination of undernutrition caused by the withdrawal of milk (for such cultures do not have milk supplies for the weaning) and the depression of the child who is being weaned forcefully by her mother. It is a psychosomatic disease. In India, a child is not considered to be a "real" person until she has made it past this hurdle at the end of the second year. Such beliefs protect responsible adults from feeling devastated by their sense of inadequacy as parents.

In the United States, the issues around feeding are likely to be different on the surface, but the underlying issues are not. Mothers still feel it is their responsibility to see that their babies are fed. With the availability of all kinds of food, the choice of "which is best" becomes the issue. In my practice in Cambridge mothers read all they can about food and feeding. Their concerns, their anger, their conflict is engendered by fears about contaminants in food, food additives, vitamins, and radioactivity in milk from fallout. All these fears reflect the extent of the mothers' feelings of responsibility. They feel it is up to them to provide the best—not just adequate—food for their babies and children. As one mother said, "I feel that if I feed my baby properly, he can become president. If I don't, he may become a bum." This statement shocked me because of its intensity, but it reflects the underlying desire to give a baby the best possible start. Being a good mother quickly becomes equated with being a good provider of food.

GETTING STARTED

To breastfeed or not is the first big decision about feeding. Most pediatricians, if not all, feel that it is preferable to bottle feeding for most babies. Not only is breast milk loaded with protective antibodies against infection, but it is much more digestible and less allergenic than the best formula made. If a woman can breastfeed, it is to the baby's advantage. But there are unconscious as well as physical reasons which may interfere with a new mother's success. Her own experience may have been such that she is turned against it or feels inadequate to the task. If a mother who feels this way doesn't get support from people around her, she is likely to fail at the attempt to breastfeed. In my experience, with real emotional and physical support, most women can make a go of it. The pleasure they derive when they succeed is a real boost to their feelings of success as a mother. When breastfeeding goes well, a mother has a real chance to learn the rhythms, the temperament, the feel of her new baby.

Fathers should try to find a time to feed the baby once a day or at least twice a week. In the feeding situation, the chance to feel closeness and intimacy is nonesuch. A successful feeding followed by a successful bubble gives any parent a real thrill. I always warn fathers that if their babies are on the breast and are having to work hard to get milk, they will have learned to be very efficient suckers. On a bottle, they will gulp it down so quickly and efficiently that it may well act like an elevator. Down too quickly and up it will come, a bubble bringing back the whole feeding. Hence, a father should be sure his baby takes the bottle *as slowly as possible* by using a nipple with a small hole.

John and Mary Lincoln had shared her pregnancy as thoroughly as they could. He'd participated with Mary in labor and was elated at the delivery. The perfect little girl certainly felt to him as if she were partly his. What he hadn't been prepared for was how awed he was by her. As he stood over her to watch her breathe, he jumped whenever she started in her sleep. When she was awake, he dared not touch her, so fragile did she seem to him. The first chance he had to hold her without someone nearby to help occurred on the third day. His wife had left her bed to go to the bathroom. No one was nearby when baby Karen let out a cry. John ran quickly for a nurse but no one came. Karen continued to stir and began to fuss insistently. He had no choice. He had to pick her up. She felt to him like a bundle of wiggling extremities. Legs, arms, body all seemed to fly off in different directions. He struggled to contain her. Finally he remembered that the nurses always wrapped her before they lifted her. After this, they could move her around in one piece. He felt triumphant as she lay quilted, wrapped and cuddled in his arms.

This experience confirmed his resolve to feed her. Mary was successfully feeding her at the breast by the time they brought her home on the fourth day. They looked cozy as a nursing couple and John realized he was jealous of them both. He and Mary had discussed his participation beforehand, and it seemed the time was coming for him to try her with a bottle so that Mary could sleep a bit at night. By the sixth day, Mary's milk was firmly established. Their doctor encouraged him to take a nighttime feeding. When Karen cried at one in the morning, he realized he'd been only half asleep, waiting in eager anticipation. Mary groaned and began to rise up in the bed. He whispered to her, "Let me do this one," as he rushed to beat Mary to Karen. He got her out of her crib, realizing that she was wet and dirty, as well as hungry. She would need to be changed as well. Which came first—the feeding or the diaper change? He'd forgotten. He called to his wife who'd gone thankfully back to sleep. She mumbled, "Change her" from her sleep. So John attempted to put her down. Her wails increased as he put her on the changing table. He picked her up and hurried over to the kitchenette to place her already prepared bottle in warm water. Then he changed her, ignoring her wails, her moving arms and legs. When he finally had her wrapped up safely, he sat down to feed her the ready bottle.

As he sat with her, he rocked gently, listening to her loud gulps with satisfaction. At last he was doing something for this little creature. Suddenly, all of his fantasies of becoming a parent began to seem as if they were becoming real. He felt as if he were a father! Karen gulped down the entire bottle in record time. John remembered too late that he'd neglected to stop her in the middle to burp her. But she'd at least gotten it all—and he felt proud. As he put her on his shoulder to burp her, she began to squirm. He rocked harder. After a minute or so, her face wrinkled, her legs came up to flex on her abdomen, and she let out an enormous burping noise. The whole feeding followed rapidly, literally shooting across the room.

He was covered with her spit-up milk. It had hit the wall behind him. He looked at the exhausted baby in his arms, as she recovered from this effort. She lay limp in his arms. He felt like weeping. All of this effort had been in vain for them both. Had he hurt her? Was she all right? His immediate response was to call out in pain. His next was to hide it all, to act as if it had never happened. He wiped up the milk, from her, from himself, from the room around them. Gently, he laid her in her crib and crept quietly into his own bed. He stared at the ceiling for the next three hours, waiting for her to cry, to show Mary what a failure he was.

After a rapid, gulped feeding, prop the infant at a 30° angle for a 20–30-minute period before bubbling her. In that time, gravity will push the milk down, bringing the lighter bubble to the top of the stomach. Then when the baby is held upright, the bubble will come up without the milk. This is important for fathers who are helping out nursing mothers, because if each feeding ends with failure, they will feel more and more like a failure with the baby.

The area of feeding is a critical learning area for new parents. They know they must get an adequate amount of food into the baby. In order to do this, they may overdo it, by feeding her whenever she wakens or whenever she fusses. In the initial adjustment period at home, it is probably necessary for new parents to feed each time the baby cries. But as they learn about the infant's cycles from one state of consciousness to another—sleep and alert periods—it becomes critical to push the baby to fill up her time with experiences beside feeding. Playing in her crib alone, watching her hands, or playing with the adults around her, learning about her world, soon become as critical as feeding. By 3 or 4 weeks of age, parents should start to separate feeding times from other important experiences. The baby's need to learn about herself and to explore her new world already needs to be balanced with the need for food. Parents must learn to respect this balance, but it is difficult. In these periods the baby begins to show independence.

ROADBLOCKS

Mothers feel that if they provide food, the baby should eat it. If not, getting it down the baby becomes the issue. When the child resists her proffered food, it first amazes, then sets up anger in a mother. How can she not want to eat? Is it something I am doing wrong? A grandmother in my office sat rocking while I explained to her daughter-in-law that she must not push food into her year-old baby. As I explained my arguments, the mother-in-law rocked harder, shaking her head from side-to-side. I felt as if my arguments were wasted, for I was sure that this negative old lady would undermine them as soon as they left my office. Finally, she spoke up to say, "Doctor, I wish I had heard that when I was raising my children. We were taught the phrase *"Essen und brechen,"* meaning "Eat and vomit" in Yiddish. A mother's repsonsibility was to make her child eat. It didn't matter what happened to the food afterward!" This grandmother understood that the drive to get food down the baby can make mothers struggle against the independence of the child. When she hits a period of independence and won't eat for her, most new mothers feel deserted and angry.

Is it any wonder that such a roadblock looms large and detracts from the mother's own image of herself at a time when it is critical that she feel like *the* perfect mother? In our culture, most women are inexperienced in mothering small babies. There is usually no extended family to support them in such apparently unimportant crises. The only backup is likely to be from the media, which tend to perpetuate the idealized mother, implicitly decrying the less-than-ideal. A mother is likely to see herself as a massive failure when she recognizes any deviation from this ideal.

Kenneth Kaye, Professor of Education at the University of Chicago, and I saw that one of the first of these roadblocks for mothers who were learning to feed their new babies might come from the baby herself. We were aware that a baby would suck constantly when she started on the bottle or breast, but after an initial burst of sucks, she would fall into a burst-pause pattern. A burst of eight or ten sucks would be followed by a pause of a few seconds before the next burst continued. This rhythmic pausing pattern seemed to concern mothers, and they automatically would juggle the baby, or reach down to touch her cheek, or look down to speak to her. If we asked her why she did this, she said, "I want to keep her going, so she will take a good feeding." Since we saw that the burst-pause pattern was a universal one, we clocked the duration of the pauses when a group of mothers did try to shorten the pause and when they ignored it. To our surprise, the unattended pauses were shorter than the pauses in which the mothers responded. In other words, the babies prolonged the pauses when their mothers answered them with a social response, as if the communication with the mother during the pauses were as important as the feeding itself. The mother's agenda was to get the baby to eat, but the baby's agenda was to mix feeding with positive social experience.

Feeding provides many opportunities for mothers and babies to learn about each other. Unconsciously for the most part, they test each other's limits during a feeding. With each spurt of development, tensions are likely to increase between them, and will influence the feeding climate. It is a good idea not to let this area become a contest. I now expect that mothers in my practice will at certain times complain to me about their babies' feedings. The times are always associated with bursts in the baby's increasing awareness of herself and of her environment. They are spurts in her independence—even in infancy.

At 4-1/2 or 5 months, a baby's horizon suddenly widens. She has learned to reach for objects, and this increases her interest in everything around her. Sights, sounds, objects take on new meaning and she can hardly spare the time to settle down to a feeding. If there is any noise in the vicinity, if a sibling moves into sight, her interest in feeding ceases and she turns to look or listen. Mothers tend to blame this on teething, or to worry about loss of appetite. But, in truth, it is the result of a burst of new interest in the world. If feeding takes place in a quiet, darkened room where stimuli are at a minimum, the baby will eat better. But the main thing for the mother to realize is that such a period of refusal is normal and temporary. She'll start eating again in a few weeks if they don't get locked into a struggle. If the mother is breastfeeding, her milk may begin to decrease. I recommend taking the baby into a quiet dark room for a feeding at least twice a day—morning and evening—to avoid losing precious breast milk.

FOOD VS. ADVENTURE

At 7 or 8 months, as she begins to be better able to manipulate objects with her fingers, a baby becomes completely involved in exploring her world with her hands. She enjoys a feeling of mastery with her fingers that can fill up her whole day. She pokes, she pulls, she pushes, she uses her new-found fingers in a endless ballet. She wants to master her whole world. This, of course, becomes the time to introduce finger foods. Unless she can participate actively in a feeding, she will feel a real conflict of interest. If she can hold onto a piece of toast or a cookie, she can be a participant. If she can work to master her new pincer grasp of forefinger and thumb by picking up a pea or a Cheerio, she will feel the whole meal has been worth it. While she is working at this important new task, she can be fed a whole meal. If this new developmental area is ignored, it can easily lead to a feeding problem.

Over the next few months the baby's desire to feed herself will increase. One young mother, describing her 10-month-old baby's resistance to being fed, told me proudly that the only way she could feed him was as follows: She sat the baby in front of their television set. When she wanted him to open his mouth, she would turn up the television so loud that it startled him. As he jumped, his arms would go up, his mouth opened wide. Then his mother would stuff in several spoonsful before he could close his mouth again. As he clamped his lips down to swallow rather than choke on the mouthful, she turned it up again to startle him into another mouth opening. Thus, the feeding proceeded with bursts of startles. It had not occurred to her that there were other ways to interest him in his feeding. It would have been much better had she allowed the baby his own independence. He might well have cut down for awhile on how much he ate. That wouldn't really matter, for the independence was more important than the food to the baby. A mother can see to it that important foods are provided as little bits of finger-sized pieces, one at a time. The baby then can learn about using her fingers while she goes about the job of eating. She will eat what is necessary.

The burst in independence which occurs at the end of the first year is likely to set the ground for more feeding difficulties. The baby's new-found freedom in walking brings such choices as whether to walk away from her mother or to walk toward her, whether to cooperate with her or to resist. This new sense of autonomy invades all the important events of her day. Many babies are negativistic at this time, have temper tantrums, explore new places and new experiences of all kinds. Unless parents have established feeding as the baby's territory, not theirs, food is likely to become a prime focus for struggle over autonomy. The pleasure in being a parent has been fed by the blissful reciprocity of the first year. When the baby begins to feel her oats and to pull away, any parent's instinct is to hold on tighter. A mother who has seen herself exclusively as a good provider will be dominated by the "Essen und brechen" philosophy. She will feel that the baby's autonomy in feeding is a threat to her good mothering. As the baby sits there deciding whether or not to eat the food she has prepared, she is likely to feel threatened. Mothers say to me, "I realized she didn't care as much about her food as she used to, so I made it more tasty. I went to a lot more trouble over her meal, and then she wouldn't eat it. It feels like she is rejecting me when she turns down my food!" This is missing the point. She is learning about herself, and that is more critical to the baby at this point than eating her food. If a mother presses her to eat, she will become all the more determined to have her own way.

KEEPING OUT OF THE STRUGGLE

Nearly every baby goes through massive changes in feeding habits in the second year. By 15 months many toddlers are refusing all vegetables for one month, meat the next month, milk the third. As one set of refusals take precedence, the last one decreases in its value to the child—*unless* the parents have become involved and are pressing the child to eat. If they are involved, refusals of various foods can become more and more exciting to the child, and each meal becomes a battle. The child is experiencing a rewarding response to her normal negativity; the parent is feeling hopelessly beaten and inadequate. I have seen this build up so subtly that the whole relationship becomes endangered, and the angry tension between parents and child starts to go beyond food. This, then, is the way a feeding problem gets started—not because parents do not care or are "bad" parents, but because they care too much. It starts when autonomy or independence begin to surface in the baby, and centers on the mutual area of concern and caring—the area of feeding.

Maria was just under a year when she found that dropping a toy over the side of her chair was a sure way to capture her parents. As if by chance at first, she would casually drop her toy, then a few insistent whines brought her parents to her. If they'd give it back to her, she'd drop it over and over until they tired of her game. Since she was learning all about disappearing objects and how to hide and retrieve them, they were charmed by her game for quite a period.

When she found that she could play this game with her food and her feeding utensils, her parents were less charmed. At first, they tried to ignore her with cool silence. Next, they began to be firm in their effort to stop her playing with food! "Maria, stop that. You cannot play with your food." Maria obviously was not distinguishing between the toy game and the game of manipulating her parents with food. The fact that they reacted so strongly and so predictably made it even more exciting.

Maria began to make mealtimes a continual game time. She dropped the solid foods. She began to smear mushy food. All this brought out predictable, strong reactions in her parents. She drank milk out a cup, and handled her cup all alone. She would finish off a few ounces, then pour the rest onto her tray table to make a better mush. When her mother tried to spank her hand or to reprimand her, she began to throw bits of food. Meanwhile, she was up and down in her chair, standing up in it to deliver an ovation. Maria's mother was desperate.

The pediatrician came to her rescue. He explained that this was an area where Maria knew she could provoke her parents into predictable reactions. Since this was the beginning of a normal period of negativism for her, their reactions were rewards on which she thrived. He suggested that they give her just a few bits of food at a time, and an ounce of milk in her cup. When she began to play with them, they were to take them away before she began to tease. Then her meal would be at an end. The inevitable teasing that was part of this developmental stage need not invade the feeding area. But, he warned her mother, Maria might not eat very much food, and she would beg for food in between meals. Her doctor advised her parents to hold the mealtimes sacred, and not to feed her "snacks" in between. Otherwise, her sensitivity to her mother's desire to feed her would lead her to provoke her parents into compromises about feeding which they'd regret later. He reiterated the foods which would cover her minimal requirements through this period. Since she was on three bottles, he suggested that her mother beat up a raw egg in one of them to make a milkshake if she began to refuse other protein. With the bottles, her liquid vitamins and the egg or any small amount of iron-containing protein, her minimum requirement would be met.

The only solution is to get out of the struggle. You won't win and you really shouldn't. The baby's independence is too important. Even if you did win, by pure might, the feeding area would become charged and future problems would be likely to arise in that area. If you can see food as an area where the baby's own independence and the rewards of new learning are likely to surface, or conversely if you can understand that learning and exploring independence will almost certainly take place in the feeding situation, you will be able to take the baby's resistance less personally. In our country, babies are well-enough established in the first year to survive nutritionally through many bouts of negativism about food in the second or third year. If you can remember that only four basic ingredients (see below) will provide a baby with enough to maintain her through the most rebellious periods, you can allow her the necessary freedom to explore, to refuse, to test limits. In the third or fourth year, she will begin to eat again and your restraint will be rewarded.

Make yourself some rules. For instance, you know a toddler will tease you by playing with her food. Dropping it over the side of the table to see whether you'll pick it up is fun and it's good for the end of every meal. Hence, set it up so you don't get caught. Feed a few bits at a time. Too much in the dish or on the tray is a real challenge. Of course, a baby will throw food around. The manipulation of food coupled with this kind of teasing is a lot more exciting than eating. If you stop the feeding immediately when such play begins, a toddler soon will learn that food is not a play area. Ultimately, she will become more serious and respectful of mealtime.

For the same reasons, have limits on how long you expect her to sit at the table. No active toddler will want to stay immobilized and sitting for too long. And yet it is important that she learn eventually that adults sit down for meals. I do not feel that getting her to eat more is important enough to justify allowing a toddler to walk around while eating. I personally feel that a toddler must learn to separate the rituals of mealtime from the rest of the day. I do not like to see a baby walking around with a bottle hanging out of her mouth, or pieces of food in one hand as she plays with a toy with the other. Children are likely to tease parents to break their rituals, but observing them is important to the whole family. And if a child is expected to sit to eat—even for a short time—she will learn the importance of the ritual. The amount of food consumed at such a teasing, provocative time will certainly not be great. But quantity of food is not the issue. The rituals of the family must be measured against the baby's natural inclinations to explore, to test, to provoke anxiety and anger in the parents. Feeding is an area in which the child knows she can get reactions from her parents. Unless a parent is aware of this, mealtime will indeed become a subtle, and then not-so-subtle battleground.

This is difficult advice to follow unless the parents have already decided that feeding should be a pleasant communicative area. That is the ultimate goal. At certain times, the struggle for autonomy will peak and will invade the feeding area. But, as in other aspects of childrearing described in this book, limits and rules around feeding help a child learn to set her own limits and give her a kind of security. If caring parents can remind themselves that a baby will survive nutritionally, and that her total development may be more critical than a perfect diet, feeding need not develop into a battleground.

MINIMUM DAILY REQUIREMENTS

Knowing how modest the child's requirements are in the second or third year can help parents relax. The four ingredients as daily requirements I have advised over the years are simple ones—and there are simple substitutes when even these are refused:

1. A pint (16 ounces) of milk or its equivalent in cheese, yogurt, ice cream. Flavored milk works when you are desperate. A teaspoon of liquid calcium (Neocalglucon) is equivalent to 8 ounces of milk. This can be mixed into any drink the baby happens to prefer at the moment.
2. A total of 4 ounces of meat. or an egg provides adequate iron and protein. If these are refused, an iron-protein supplement can be prescribed by your doctor.
3. An ounce of fruit juice or of fresh fruit in any form provides vitamin C.
4. A multivitamin preparation (with or without fluoride for teeth, depending upon the availability in natural foods or water) which contains A, B, and C vitamins will cover the ingredients of vegetables and cereals. Since vegetables become a likely target for refusals, I use vitamins in the second year as a "crutch"—in order to forget about them.

GUIDELINES

To keep mealtimes from being a struggle, a parent might try these suggestions:

1. Have regular feeding times, and no snacks in between.

2. Expect a maximum time of 20 minutes at the table. After that, put the toddler down and put away the food.

3. Give small amounts of food at a time. When the child finishes these, furnish more. As soon as the toddler begins to play with her food, end the meal.

4. Avoid too much emphasis on food by not trying to find out what the child will eat or what she wants. Although she may lead you from one food to another, it may not be another food she is really after, but the excitement which provocative behavior engenders.

9
SLEEP

"How can I make my baby sleep?" is a question I am asked at least once a day in my practice. The question usually is phrased in terms of the parents' survival, for by the time my advice is sought, there has been a long history of nighttime turmoil—one or the other parent waking up at 2:00 or 3:00 a.m., dragging herself or himself to the child, and then rocking, singing, cajoling to try to get the child back to bed.

The child, on the other hand, is winning, delightful, and full of charm; he has had his sleep and is ready for several hours of play. When his charm begins to fail in the face of his parent's desperation, he may fall back on whimpering or wailing as if he were in real pain Or he may stare accusingly at the parent with a look that seems to say, "How can you leave me alone when you can see how much I want you to stay?"

If these wiles do not seem to be succeeding, he may become anxious, as if he is frightened of the anger he is calling up in these usually loving adults. At any level, the urgent message he conveys is that he has needs that have not yet been fulfilled, and such a message reaches across any self-protective barrier the sleepy parent may attempt to set up.

Parents tell me they "try everything." They even try letting the child "cry it out," but they give up this approach after a few nights when the crying goes on for one or two hours and shows no signs of stopping. They try giving him a bottle and a nightlight; neither works. But taking him into their bed does—he can sit there and play for an hour or two, and at least they can sleep.

Because there is an unwritten taboo in our culture against allowing a child into his parents' bed, many mothers and fathers work very hard to deny themselves such an easy solution. They have found that going to the child before he is upset shortens the period of calming down afterward. They often tell me that they go to him every two hours after 2:00 a.m., quieting him, giving him milk, rocking him for a period and successfully keeping him in his room. They can time their visit so well that they only have to remain with him for 30 minutes out of every two hours, whereas if they waited until he was upset and wailing, the visit would take an hour!

What is the problem here? Why don't all children make such demands? Why is it that in one family all but one child learns to sleep through the night? Is it a sign of insecurity on the child's part? Is it a sign to the parents that he had not had enough love or attention during the day? Why is it that most babies who go to sleep at 6:00 p.m. regularly awaken and make demands on their parents at about 10:00 p.m.?

SLEEP CYCLES

Perhaps an understanding of the development of sleep cycles in early infancy will provide the answers to some of these questions. According to recent studies by Drs. Arthur H. Parmeles, Jr., of U.C.L.A., Thomas F. Anders of Stanford University, and Robert N. Emde of the University of Colorado, every infant has characteristic cycles of light and deep sleep during the night. Over the first few months, the periods of deep sleep become longer and the light, or dreaming, periods become shorter.

By the age of 4 months the periods begin to get set into a pattern—usually a cycle lasting three or four hours. In the middle of the cycle there is an hour to an hour and a half of deep sleep in which the baby moves very little and is difficult to rouse with any stimulation. For an hour on each side there is a lighter, dreaming state in which activity comes and goes. And at the end of each four-hour cycle, the baby comes up to a semi-alert state in which he is very close to consciousness and awakens easily. At these times each baby has his own activity pattern—he may suck his fingers, cry out, rock himself, or bang his head rhythmically. (One of our daughters would recount her whole day to her doll every four hours.) He may fuss or talk to himself, or he may call out to his parents.

All of this behavior seems to serve the purpose of discharging energy stored up from daytime activities and of getting the child back down into the next cycle of sleep. When these intervals of semiconsciousness can be managed by the baby himself, the sleep cycles become stabilized, and the child begins to stretch them into longer cycles, so that he finally manages to stay asleep for eight and even 12 hours at a time.

Current researchers have shown that the prolongation of these cycles depends upon conditioning by the environment. If the infant is in an environment that reinforces each alert period by a visit or by a feeding, he is not likely to stretch out the sleeping hours by settling down by himself. But if the environment is unresponsive, he will be pressed to find his own patterns for discharging activity and comforting himself back down into the next cycle.

The same researchers have also demonstrated that 24-hour rhythms are already entrenched at birth having been established in synchrony with the pregnant woman's own daily cycles. They usually are not parallel to the maternal cycle, since the fetus sleeps while the mother is active and wakes when she lies down. But her activity period leads to his in the following period. The newborn infant has a sleep-wake rhythm already. After birth the environment tends to press the new baby to more and more wakefulness in the daytime and to longer and longer sleep cycles in the night.

Certain children—but the number is surprisingly small—start out as if their cycles were reversed. Parents usually try to press them to change, and most infants begin to sleep for an eight-hour stretch at night by 5 or 6 months of age. To me, this is prime evidence of the infant's inborn ability to be shaped by his environment.

The few infants who do not respond to the subtle but firm demands of the environment have always interested me, and I have tried to study a few of them in order to see what the ingredients of their failure may be—for it is indeed a failure as far as the parents are concerned, since their own needs for sleep are being violated.

Most children begin to sleep longer than four hours without waking by the age of 3 months, and a study of normal sleeping in our present society confirms this. According to this research 70% of American children sleep eight hours a night by 3 months and 83% are likely to be doing this by 6 months; by one year only 10% do not sleep through the night.

Why do most children seem to sleep through? It is likely that there is a combination of influences that successfully encourages most babies into a long stretch at night. These infuences range from the parents' effort not to "bother" them at night to the child's own need to stretch out in some part of the 24-hour cycle.

CAUSES OF NIGHT WAKING

Which babies make up the 17% who aren't stretching out at night by 6 months, and the 10% who still aren't sleeping at 1 year? Again, a combination of factors is likely to be involved. On the one hand, there may be parents who don't want to give the baby up to sleep in his own room and in his own bed and who are quick to offer their bed as an alternative. (If he doesn't sleep well there either, they might be more able to ignore him than if they were lying in bed, feeling guilty, in another room.) On the other hand, there are babies of three different temperamental types who seem prone to night waking.

One kind is very active, intensely driving, and has such excitement for learning that he is literally unable to stop himself when he is learning a new task. At night the frustration of not being able to accomplish the task he's got in mind—usually a motor achievement such as standing or walking—seems to drive him as intensely as it does during the day. For example, shortly before he begins to walk, when he comes to a state of semiconsciousness, he may get up on his hands and knees to rock in frustration, or he may pull up on his crib endlessly—and then he will awaken. Waking at night is all a part of the intensity that marks every new developmental milestone.

Unfortunately, this pattern may not subside after walking is achieved unless the parents begin to intervene by pressing the child to master his nighttime sleep pattern. He may be as frustrated about other tasks and other steps toward mastery in the second, third, and later years; and if sleep has become an outlet for frustration in the first year, it may continue to serve this purpose. When one of these babies comes up to REM or light sleep, he awakens and needs help.

If parents do sleep with these children in order to comfort them, they must realize that these REM sleep cycles occur frequently during the night and are self-limited *as long as* the child can quiet himself and then bring himself down into deeper sleep again. If he is too stimulated by his parents' presence or if he uses their presence to wake up and start playing, he may indeed turn night into day, and a vicious circle may easily be set in motion. The child awakens; the parents become tense as they try to quiet him, inevitably adding their stimulation to the child's own, thereby rousing him further; the child senses his parents' hostile feelings and stays awake to tease or play with them or to try to establish a bond with them. This pattern will neither comfort the child nor add to the parents' capacity to nurture him during the day.

Another group of infants who may wake at night and need to be comforted could be classified as "low motor expenders" during the day. They are the quiet, alert, watchful children who take everything in and think deeply about it and may not be very active. They don't invest a lot of activity in their daylight hours, so they don't tire themselves enough to sleep as deeply at night. Their sensitive thinking processes may be patterned to increase wakefulness at night, and when REM cycles occur, they may easily become wide awake. If they cry out or fuss in each of these cycles, they may benefit from the comfort of their parents' bed. As long as both they and the parents benefit from this kind of closeness, it might serve them all. But as the child's independence in the second year surfaces, it will be a time to consider pushing him to be more independent at night.

The third kind of baby who may find it difficult to settle down at night into a reliably prolonged sleep pattern is the child who tends to be sensitive and easily upset. His sensitivity to new or strange situations makes him rather clinging, and his parents may play into this unknowingly. Around each new demanding situation—either a new developmental step or a demanding social situation—he is likely to regress during the day as well as at night. Since the parents of such a child want to help him, they may protect him from new and demanding situations. They are likely to hasten to comfort him when he is overwhelmed, often before he has had the chance to try out his own efforts at coping. In the process they may transmit to him a feeling that he cannot cope, that he is indeed inadequate in meeting the demands of a new situation. He begins to see himself as helpless and becomes more sensitive and more dependent as a result.

When the child wakes up at night, the pattern of overprotection is likely to affect the behavior of both parents and child. The child demands their presence and comfort long after he may really need it, and the parents in turn find it difficult not to give in. They may take him into their bed or allow him to ask for and receive four or five nighttime visits from them. As they get exhausted and angry—with themselves and with him—his sensitivity to their ambivalence increases his frantic demands, and his parents' very ambivalence drives them on to meet all his demands.

I have repeatedly been surprised and gratified when parents have consulted me about such a child. When they can accept what I tell them and can press him to be more autonomous at night by giving him a "lovey"—a substitute for them that reinforces his autonomy—it has surprised them how ready he is to stay by himself. And it also surprises them when he begins to feel and act more independently during the day as well.

CULTURAL EXPECTATIONS

Certainly issues of autonomy and independence are often at the root of sleep problems. In part, this results from the fact that in our society, although there are many forces that press a parent to feel guilty about holding a child too close or too long, most parents are not quite ready to push a baby of 5 or 6 months into separate living and sleeping quarters unless he accepts them readily. As the baby gets older, there are easy rationalizations for parents that back up the natural feelings of wanting to cling and to be clung to. Surely most parents secretly long for the lovely warm comfort of a sleeping baby next to them. Why, then, does our society demand such early separation at night? There is now a counter trend, marked by a book, *The Family Bed,** by Tine Thevenin, to have the entire family in one large bed.

In parts of India, I am told, the mother sleeps on a large, circular mat on the floor. All her small children move on and off the mat with her at will during the night. She never stirs. No sleep problems are reported. The folk wisdom says that a child will separate from the mother of his own accord in his fourth year; until then he is too little and helpless to be expected not to want her at night.

In Mayan Mexico, where my family and I lived for awhile, I observed that the mother slept with her baby next to her, between her and her husband, until the child was suddenly directed to his own bed. This abrupt expectation that he sleep alone across the hut, together with the cessation of continuous breast feeding and being carried on the mother's back all day, came in the middle of the second year. If the child murmured about any of these moves, he was ignored or punished. If he became depressed, stopped eating, and developed a syndrome of malnutrition called *kwashiorkor,* it was attributed to a sickness that many, many children pass through. No one connected the sudden taking away of maternal comforts with his depression and

---

*Minneapolis, Minnesota, 1977.

undernutrition. No one could afford to, for it came about when the next baby was imminent, and there was no longer any room for the older child in the bed.

In our culture we expect independence and individuality, resilience and curiosity as well as early achievement—and these expectations motivate many of our child-rearing practices. We expect our babies to be active and inquisitive during the day and independent at night. An ideal baby is one who can play all day, mostly alone, but who also can accept nurture when it is offered on the adult's terms. At night he is supposed to give up, subsiding quickly and single-mindedly to sleep.

All of us can understand the way a baby teases when he first goes to bed. We know we are being conned when we go in with water or the pot for the first, fifth, or sixth time, and we take it pretty much in stride. But we do not find it easy or even tolerable to be awakened at night, except in rare and dire cases. So, when a parent is regularly deprived of a night of continuous sleep, he or she must deal with negative feelings toward the child. In order to handle these feelings and not express them directly to the baby, one must develop pretty strong defenses. The parents of a child with a real sleeping problem build up reasons in their minds to explain why they should respond to their child's needs for them during the night. This trend is increasing in our culture, as more women work during the day and feel a need for the baby at night. Many parents now believe it is all right for a child of any age, whether infant or four-year-old, to sleep in their bed as a way of avoiding sleep problems, but they are still sensitive to criticisms of their friends and of society around them. None of the parents in my practice will admit to me that they routinely allow their baby in bed with them. Why not? They may feel that I shall try to talk them out of it. But more important, I think it may be because they themselves are unconsciously guilty about it. If they are, their ambivalence about such a practice will pass itself onto the child and he may suffer. He may not understand why, but he will begin to feel guilty about sleeping with his parents at a time when he is likely to be unable to change such a habit for himself.

In our society, at least, to be able to sleep alone in childhood is a part of being an independent person. Whether or not that is right can certainly be questioned, but it is difficult at this time for a child or a parent to reject the general consensus of society without the danger of lowered self-esteem and a feeling of being inadequate to the job of establishing autonomy.

SLEEP AND THE
DEVELOPMENT OF AUTONOMY

In the first year, there are predictable times when a baby is likely to start waking at night, even though he may have been sleeping through before. At 8–9 months and again at a year, there are rapid increases in cognitive awareness (of strangers or strange situations, of new places, of changes in the daily routine) that are coincident with spurts in motor development (such as crawling and sitting at 8 months; standing, walking, and climbing at 12–14 months) (see Chapter 3). With this increased activity comes a new capacity for getting away from the safe base of mother and father.

The choice between moving away from his parents or staying with them creates a kind of dissonance that can disturb an infant. He wants the independence and at the same time is frightened by the prospect of it. This dissonance leaves him upset at the end of the day. During the night, when he comes to a cycle of light sleep, he shows his disequilibrium by crying out and often by getting up to stand in his bed.

Learning to sleep alone at night is certainly tied to the job of learning about independence. When sleep problems occur, it is likely that both parents and child are having difficulties in feeling that the child can make it alone. Mothers who work away from home during the day can almost invariably expect a sleep problem along the way. When it can be talked about, I have found that the mother feels torn about the sharing of job and mothering. When a natural stress event comes along that produces a period of waking in the child, she is likely to find it hard to press the child to separate from her at night.

Judy Trail, a gentle but rather tense young woman, was in my office with her husband Tom and their 18-month-old Lucy. Before she became pregnant the first time, Judy had been the executive secretary to a prominent lawyer. She and Tom had been married three years when they decided they wanted a baby. But the pregnancy ended in miscarriage at three months, and both Judy and Tom were surprised at the disappointment each of them felt. To have lost their baby was a real blow.

Judy became rather driven to be pregnant again, and when she found that she was, she and Tom planned each move thereafter with obsessive precision. She took "perfect" care of herself and gave up her job when she was six months pregnant in order not to endanger her chances of completing the last trimester. After her resignation, her office kept the post available for her for nearly a year. Each time they called to see if she was ready to return, Judy was faced with another decision about her choice of roles—mother or business-woman.

Lucy was a delight. She was a pretty, appealing baby with a round body, dimpled elbows and hands, and a soft, curly mop of hair that made her look beatific. She was a "person" in Tom's and Judy's minds from the first. Although in many ways she was an easy baby, she was rather definite and made her demands incisive at all times. During the first weeks of her life she went quickly from a calm, peaceful attitude of playing on her own to a piercing, demanding cry that brought her parents to her immediately. She let Judy and Tom know in no uncertain manner when she was hungry, bored, or tired.

In the second year, with this combination of parents who wanted desperately to do the "right" thing and a strong-minded little girl, a problem arose about sleeping. Lucy began to protest when she was put to bed and when she woke during the night. Judy and Tom tried all the routines suggested by their library of baby books. They rocked her, they cuddled her, they gave her extra feedings, they sat in des-perate silence in the living room hoping their efforts had paid off, they left her lights on and turned theirs off, they lay down on a cot in her room, and finally they readjusted their own lives in order to accommodate her. She ended up in bed with them each night. None of them was sleeping. All were exhausted and at the breaking point when they came to see me.

Judy's and Tom's questions were focused upon how they could manage the bedtime problem and on Judy's latest resolution—to leave Lucy in day care or with "anyone" so that she could get back to work and to her sanity.

For Judy and Tom to understand why they were trying so hard to comply with Lucy's protests about sleeping, it became necessary for them to uncover their own complicated feelings about separating from her. Because of the infant they had lost earlier, they had uncon-scious fears that they would lose Lucy too. Although they knew it was in Lucy's best interests that she learn to comfort herself back to sleep at night, they also had the feeling—which many parents in our un-certain culture have—that somehow the child knows better than the parents what she needs, that somehow their needs must be ignored.

As we discussed these issues, Judy admitted how keenly she felt her failure to deal with Lucy and how she had been longing to run back to work to get to a place where she felt successful; and Tom revealed a great deal of hidden anger—at himself, at Lucy, and at his wife—for not being able to solve this problem. We began to discuss what these feelings of angry desperation on both their parts must mean to Lucy. She had changed, they agreed, from being a definite little girl to one who was unsure of herself and clinging, as if she were trying desperately to settle the tension she felt in her parents.

We discussed the importance of Lucy's having a solid feeling of her own strengths and her autonomy and the fact that this kind of autonomy could not be grounded in their compliance with her every demand or whim. For her to develop feelings about her own strengths she needed an awareness of limits. And the surest limits were likely to come from her parents—particularly when she began making inroads on needs of theirs.

I urged Judy and Tom to make up their minds *first* that they really wanted to help Lucy solve the sleep issue. In order to do that, they needed to see that Lucy could profit by learning to be independent at night. And they needed to agree on this first, for Lucy sensed far too easily when she upset their relationship. Nighttime is a vulnerable time for adults, and tensions run high. So they needed to agree with each other about a regime and how they would handle it, in order to be consistent with her.

If Lucy could "learn" to adopt a lovey—a doll or a special blanket or a single toy—during the day as "hers," she could begin to fall back on it when she was tired, hungry, or bored. It might well mean that Judy and Tom would have to push her to it at such times. It might be necessary to say things like, "Go get your lovey, and then you can climb up in my lap." Or "You can sit and rock with your friend while I'm fixing your dinner. You're a big girl now." When I suggested this, Judy said, "But she's got ten or twenty toys in her crib already! They don't help her." I assured Judy that ten or twenty were not the same as one special one, and I suspected that Lucy's ability to fall back on one had never really been tested. Judy admitted that she'd never really expected Lucy to be independent in the day or at night.

After the expectation had been set in the daytime and the lovey had been established as a reliable substitute for her mother, Judy and Tom could commend Lucy for her ability to comfort herself. Then they could begin to prepare her for independence at night.

The first step would be to be sure she knew that she must stay in her room and then that she must fall asleep by herself there. I suspected that this would mean that one parent would have to stay with her at first until she did fall asleep, after their bedtime ritual was finished. I recommended that it should be the one who was most determined she should learn to get herself to sleep.

After she'd learned to fall asleep in her own room, they could leave her to fall asleep without them. If she tried to get out of her bed to come to them, they must take her back to her room. As she learned to stay in her room, they could push her to fall back on her beloved object. When she woke, they should gradually leave her for five, then ten, then fifteen minutes, calling to her to find her lovey and telling her they were there but that she should get herself to sleep. At first they might have to go to her, but they must not reward her by taking her up or by playing with or feeding her. As she learned that they meant it, she would begin to learn her own routine for independently getting herself from light sleep to deep sleep. Her lovey would be a real and ever-present crutch. When she did achieve it, both she and they would feel tremendously rewarded. It was a difficult job, but the independence and the separateness which they would establish at night would be more than compensated for in the daytime. Parents and child would thrive on an adequate night's sleep.

Our work in my office centered around the job of getting Judy and Tom to agree to back each other up. It was decided that Tom would put Lucy to bed at night, Judy would go to her the first time, and Tom the second. When they'd made up their minds to agree on a routine, Lucy seemed to sense it. She called her doll "Mawy," and Mawy became her constant companion. Mawy began to serve her purpose at night about two weeks later. Tom called me a week after they started pushing Lucy at night to say it seemed like a miracle. She'd accepted Mawy as a substitute and seemed more relieved than they that she could get herself to sleep and could stay in bed when she woke. She'd stopped calling for them after four nights, and everyone was sleeping soundly. It did seem miraculous, but I knew that once the tensions between them were resolved the sleep problem was likely to take care of itself. Tom added that Lucy seemed more grown up and proud of herself than they'd had any right to expect. Lucy's learning to sleep had been a growing process for all of them.

THE FAMILY BED

In my private pediatric practice and in my hospital work, I have seen the problems that can be stirred up in whole families when a child is awake and demanding during the night. I knew these families needed help, and I knew it would help their relationship with their child if I could give them a base for understanding the issues that come into play. What I didn't realize was how many parents did *not* believe in helping a child to learn to sleep alone at night.

These parents feel that sleeping alone is a custom our society unreasonably demands of its small children and that it isn't *necessarily* to the chldren's advantage. And they state that not only do they disagree with the principle of having a child sleep alone at night, but that when a child needs them at night, they feel it more important to be with him than to worry about conforming to any rule, right or not. They say the child's presence in their bed does not bother them and that, in fact, they and he really like being together as a family at night. What's more, they assure me that the child outgrows the habit of sleeping with his parents—without psychological scars—and they quote older children who have already done so. In short, these readers do not see night waking as a problem but instead see the separation from the child at night as a possible contributor to such a problem.

I was impressed and have learned a great deal from this point of view. First of all, I hear the reasonableness in what these parents are saying. I agree with their concern that sleep problems may indicate the child is going through a time of stress and that deserting the child at that time might not always be the best way of dealing with the problem. And I, too, feel uneasy about whether our culture isn't demanding a great deal of small children. But I also believe that the needs of the parents at night have to be considered in addition to the parents' ultimate goal for the child—autonomy and the ability to become self-reliant. If their issues can be faced squarely, I see every reason to attend to the questions that are raised by these parents.

When I wrote an article on sleep for *Redbook* magazine, some specific points were made by parents in response to my suggestion that parents could soften the blow of separating from the child at night by offering him a "lovey" or an object as a substitute for their presence. One reader wrote, "If you program our child to relate to things, to depend on things, to value things more than people, should we be surprised when that pattern continues into adulthood?"

Parents pointed out that in many other cultures the child has easy access to his parents' bed. Mrs. Kendall Keutzer of La Moille, Illinois, expressed a point of view shared by many when she wrote, "Is it not sad that a parent's sense of self-esteem could be more dependent on going along with the crowd than on doing what feels right for herself and her child? Whatever happened to autonomy and individuality in adults?"

Perhaps it is time to reevaluate our ideas on handling sleep problems in our culture. Should every family treat children alike? Do we need to press all infants and small children to separate from the family bed and to sleep alone in their own room? By following such a custom, are we furthering our stated goal of creating autonomous children, or are we pressing them toward a different kind of dependence—dependence on a "lovey" or unnecessary fears of being left alone when they are most likely to need a comforting parent? When so many parents have found that urging this early separation does not work for them and their babies, should we not reevaluate our stance? Perhaps we should.

But we should also consider some of the potential problems. Should we worry, for example, that a child will be more dependent during the day if his parents keep him close at night? I'm not sure he needs to be—but that could be a pitfall, and one I'd urge parents to watch for. If on the other hand, a child's strike for independence is going well during the day, there may be no need for this worry.

Will sharing his parents' bed as an infant and toddler make it difficult for the child to separate from them later on? Psychoanalytic theory would suggest that a child may not want to separate from his mother and father and may continue to cling to their bed and, as he gets older and his oedipal feelings get stronger, he may feel that he can come between them.

To offset this tendency on the child's part, I would urge parents who want to continue the practice of sharing their bed to be sure that they both find it comforting to them as well as to the child. His presence can certainly come between them if he's allowed to continue to sleep there; and if it does, the child will suffer more than he would have had he been weaned to his own room. Hence, if parents are not comfortable and do not agree upon this practice, I'm sure it will be destructive to a child's future development if it is allowed to become an intrusion over time. As a result, I would urge parents to discuss the arrangement openly and reasonably at regular intervals. Certainly the parents' good relationship may be more critical to a child's development than the handling of any part of his day or night.

One must also watch the child for any signs of tension about sleeping with his parents. I suspect that eventually he will begin to show that he no longer needs their comfort at night and will express a need for this kind of independence. If one can extrapolate from other cultures (India and Mexico, for example, where children in the parents' bed is a common practice), it would seem that the third or fourth year would be the time to watch for signs of the child's readiness to sleep alone, even if he hasn't been able to do this before. It will probably be up to the parents to give him the necessary encouragement—talking to the child as he goes to bed, providing him with a beloved toy for company, giving him a night light. By making the weaning process gradual, it can be an easy transition. I would worry about an older child's image of himself if he still needs to be too close to his parents at night. He may well have a more difficult separation later in childhood.

I have tried to reconsider the aspects of sleeping with an infant that may affect him in his ultimate development, in the light of the objections that many parents have raised. Meanwhile, I suspect that most parents will find it easier to expect their infants to sleep alone and to press them subtly to do so.

If this doesn't work for a particular infant and if the child or his parents are disturbed at night by his need for them, and if sharing their bed with him can solve the problem for *all of them,* they should think about it as an alternative. If on the other hand, their presence does not help him, and if it disrupts the family (I have not mentioned what it must mean to the other children when one child commandeers the parents' bed), it had better be reconsidered.

I am convinced that achieving independence of thought and action is a critical goal of childhood, and I would urge that parents consider sleep as one of the major areas in which to achieve that independence. In the end, perhaps, whether a child sleeps alone or with his parents may not be as critical as whether he is learning how to get himself back to sleep when he comes to periods of wakefulness during the night.

After 30 years in the practice of pediatrics, I am convinced that while independence may not be an easy goal for parents to accept, it is an exciting and rewarding goal for the child. Being able to manage alone at night helps the child develop a positive self-image and gives him a real feeling of strength during the day.

Need I add that instituting this kind of pressure should not be taken on at night by parents without making a real effort at increasing their child's self-respect and shoring him up emotionally during the day—and that when he does go along, he deserves all of the credit and loving praise that you can give him.

GUIDELINES

Before a child's sleep habits can be changed, both parents must be convinced that this is important. It then is wise to pick a time when the daytime stresses are minimal—when he has already mastered standing or walking, when he is not being teased by his older siblings, when he is not trying to get used to a new baby in the household, when he is not going to a new school, when he is not being toilet trained. Then parents can plan a gradual program to help a child become autonomous at night and master the job of getting himself back down from light sleep into deep sleep at regular intervals during the night.

The following suggestions might help a family reach this goal, but bear in mind that they are dependent on the individual situation and particularly the child himself. Also bear in mind that these steps should be taken singly and slowly over time.

1. The entire day must be reevaluated. Does the child sleep too long and/or too late in the afternoon? I would urge that nap times be started early (by 1:00 p.m.) and last only one to two hours at most. If the child is over two, give up the nap completely. Any rest or nap after 3:00 p.m. will certainly break up the cycle of activity and diminish the need for continuous and deep sleep during the night.

2. Be sure you have instituted a relaxing, nurturing routine at bedtime. If the child is old enough, talk to him at this time about the steps you are about to take toward helping him sleep alone and through the night.

3. Wake him at night before he wakes you. At that time you can repeat the bedtime routine—talking to him, hugging him, giving him a bottle or a feeding if that has been part of the routine. By waking him you have done two things: you have taken away his control over the situation, and you have eased your own conscience, so if and when he wakes up later, it will be difficult for you to use your old rationalizations, namely, "Is he okay? Is he hungry? Have I done enough?"

4. Reinforce a particular lovey—a blanket, an animal, even a bottle if he needs it. Later the bottle can be tied to the lovey, and when it is removed, the lovey can take its place. (Dentists are on the warpath about allowing a child to sleep with a bottleful of milk in his mouth—they say it contributes to serious tooth decay.) The lovey becomes a symbolic replacement for you; when you put him down at night and when you go to him later, you can show it to him and even push it on him. It always surprises me how readily a child can accept a lovey as a substitute. By the way, several toys in bed are in no way a reinforcement for one lovey—they dilute its value and meaning—so I would not advise a wall of toys as you institute this effort.

5. After you have prepared the child for the program and are really ready to start it, you must greet his waking with as little stimulating intervention as you can. If you have been taking him out of bed to rock him, don't; sooth and stroke him with your hand, but leave him *in bed.* He won't like it, but he'll understand. Stand by his crib and tell him that he can and must learn to get himself back to sleep.

    If he is learning to stand and won't go back down by himself, bend him in the middle to show him he can do it himself. If he gets up again, leave him standing. He'll learn quickly about letting himself down when he *knows* you mean it.

    Give him his beloved substitute for you and be sure it stays in his bed. In other words, tie it to his crib with a ribbon, for he'll throw it out and you will have to go back in to retrieve it. When he sees you mean it to be your substitute, he will accept it.

6. After a period of going to him each time, begin to stay out of his room and call to him. Tell him that you are there, that you care about him, but that you are *not* coming, and remind him of his lovey. It amazes me that a child can begin to accept one's voice for one's presence.

7. Finally, let him try all of his own resources. Wait at least 15 minutes before you go in for the first time or for a subsequent time. Then deal with him perfunctorily, repeating the unexciting regime outlined above and again pressing the lovey on him.

PART THREE

PSYCHOSOMATIC PROBLEMS

10
STOMACHACHES
AND HEADACHES

Children need to express the tensions of growing up in many ways. There are a few symptoms of such tension which appear often enough in normal children to make it worth elaborating upon them for all parents. They seem to be ways for the child to express tension or frustration or ways of seeking attention. Since these symptoms are so common and are expectable at certain ages, they are worth examining. They can become chronic psychosomatic problems, but they don't need to. They may reflect temporary stresses for the child, and a parent would be advised to listen with that in mind. They are also likely to be age-linked and an expression of the usual stresses of growing up.

Each child has an "Achilles heel"—an organ which responds to stress and creates symptoms which become the outlet for any unusual or usual pressures in the child's life. Some children get headaches, others stomachaches; still others may develop colds or a lingering croupy cough. A parent's role is to listen to the child, to be aware of the symptom as an expression of stress. If the reasons for stress can be alleviated, the parent can help in this way. If not, the symptom can be discussed with the child as her way of expressing herself under pressure. By discussing it with her, the parent will relieve the anxiety that accompanies the symptom and give the child a chance to understand herself. I never cease to be amazed at how early a child can understand herself and how important it is for her to become aware of her own mechanisms for dealing with stress. Self-awareness in a child can prevent such symptoms as headaches or stomachaches from becoming recurrent and uncontrollable psychosomatic problems.

STOMACHACHES

Laura clutched her pudgy stomach as she groaned on my examining table. She was a pretty, curly haired, blonde, 4-year-old. She had left her own birthday party to come to my office. So healthy did she look, it was hard to believe she had any dangerous obstruction in her abdomen. But her mother and I had not been able to rule it out in our two phone conversations.

Laura had had several stomachaches in the past few months. Each one seemed to get worse. They were located in the middle of her stomach, just below her rib cage. In each case, there was no obvious reason for them. There seemed to be nothing unusual that she might have eaten to have caused them. They had no real relationship to mealtime nor did they occur at any special time of the day. In each case, they lasted from one to two hours and seemed to become more violent as she and her mother worried about them. But they never were painful enough to make us decide to hospitalize her.

Mrs. Smith had called me about the first one and I asked her the questions that would help me make a decision as to whether they were serious or not. I first wanted to know whether she was constipated or had an acute infection of her intestines. Had she had a recent bowel movement? If so, was it too hard or too soft? Children at Laura's age are likely to get constipated. They often forget to go to the toilet, and even resist the urge to defecate when they are involved in play with a fascinating friend. They can often become chronically constipated without their parents being aware of it, if they continue to "forget" over a series of days. Few parents of children Laura's age watch for their children to go to the toilet. As Laura's mother said, "She's too old to hover over, and if I do, she really holds back on any urge to go to the toilet." She might have been constipated for several days. She might also eliminate liquid stool around a harder, impacted mass in her large bowel. Her mother might interpret this liquid as too soft to represent constipation. But not so. She could have constipated and liquid stools at the same time. I had instructed Mrs. Smith to look into this and had urged her to watch Laura's stools with such a possibility in mind. Mrs. Smith reassured me when she reported that she had seen a soft stool recently and she knew that Laura wasn't constipated.

I asked her mother to press on Laura's belly to see whether she was tender before she bothered to bring her to me, for many, many children of this age have belly aches. They are common, and it is often hard to know whether they are serious or not. Three maneuvers help me determine which ones need checking:

1. After a parent does her own check on the most recent bowel movement, and if she is not sure whether the pain is from a bout of constipation, it may be necessary to force the child to produce another. It is not safe to give a laxative at such a time, since that could increase the seriousness of the obstruction. So, one must consider producing one by using a suppository, if it's really a worrying enough pain. In case of an appendix or any real obstruction, it is *unlikely* that a child will be able to produce a bowel movement, even with help. An obstruction stops any passage of feces. If one is not sure whether the pain is due to a serious lesion, a suppository or an enema may become necessary to rule out such an obstruction. If there is a bowel movement afterward, it certainly rules against any real obstruction.

2. While distracting her, place your hand on her abdomen and gently press deeply all through the belly to locate the focus of any real tenderness. Her abdominal wall will automatically guard a tender area. If the pain is due to the inflammation of an appendix or another inflamed obstruction, the abdominal wall becomes irritated enough so that one cannot break through the muscle spasm. The part of the abdomen which is in trouble will be boardlike. If there is inflammation in one part of the intestine, pressure on any part of the belly, even far away from it, will cause indirect tenderness in the irritated area. Parents must distract the child and gently but persistently palpatate all through the abdomen. A child can sit in her mother's lap to watch television or be read to, to produce this distraction. If the child then continues to guard her belly and to whimper, the trouble may be serious.

3. Swollen glands from an upper respiratory infection often cause pain which mimics an obstructive bellyache. To rule these out, I try another maneuver before I see them. A buffered or plain aspirin will relieve the pain of swollen glands. Within an hour,

a parent can tell that the child's abdomen is better. With an obstruction, the aspirin would have little or no effect. Since one of the most common presenting symptoms of a cold or flu is a bellyache, this maneuver is helpful to eliminate that possibility.

Laura's first stomachache receded one hour after an aspirin, so I didn't need to see her. The next time the same thing happened. Mrs. Smith had called me each time and I'd been able to assure her that I didn't need to see her. This third time, Mrs. Smith had tried all of my suggestions—the suppository, the aspirin, and distracting her to palpate her belly. Laura continued to wail so I had to see her myself.

I had the choice of sending her directly to the hospital without seeing her. But I know what will happen if they can't be sure about her belly. If she was still tender, they'd have to X-ray and test her for evidence of an obstruction. At Laura's age, I knew she'd be worried there and might not allow them to check her properly. She trusted me and I knew I could handle her more easily than a stranger. Because the incidence of serious stomachaches is surprisingly low, I wanted to check her myself, to avoid hospitalization if possible. Only one or two a year out of many severe stomachaches in my practice ever need surgery.

I felt her belly in order to find out where her pain was located. Laura looked at me knowingly as I attempted to distract her from the pain in her belly. On my examining table, she seemed very worried about herself. She whimpered so convincingly that I felt an urgency to help her. Her mother stood watching us, with anxiety in her face. "She certainly can't be faking. She'd never leave her own birthday party to get you to examine her. She's been looking forward to her birthday for weeks! And she never got to blow out her candles, or eat her cake!" At this reminder, Laura's groaning increased in intensity. Even as I came near her, she began to wince and guarded her abdomen. So worried was she, that the muscle wall of her abdomen was too tense for me to palpate it successfully. I could not tell whether it was from pain.

I lifted Laura onto her mother's lap, holding her teddy bear. I told her I wanted to feel his belly too. I asked her to flex her legs up on her abdomen. I put my hand firmly on her belly, but without pressure. Meanwhile, I assured her that I wasn't going to hurt her and I would see that her bellyache got "fixed." She looked at me with anxiety about what I might find. When I listened with my stethoscope, I was reassured. There were bowel sounds all through her abdomen. The gurgles and growls which are a normal accompaniment to bowel activity become decreased or absent in an inflamed or obstructed area. When there is an acute appendix cooking, the bowel sounds will be absent in that area.

I asked her to hold her beloved teddy bear so I could see where his pain was. She assured me he had no stomachache. As she held him, I pressed on his sawdust-filled belly and he let out a squeak. We both laughed and I pressed him in another spot. No squeak! We both laughed harder. Meanwhile with the other hand I had been kneading her belly. As she watched me play with her teddy, couched in the safety of her mother's arms, she had relaxed. As she became distracted, I was able to palpate her abdomen, to reassure myself and her concerned mother that she was all right.

As soon as we knew she wasn't in serious trouble, we could reassure her. Almost immediately, she began to play around my office. Her active play was in great contrast to the miserable little girl who'd arrived a few minutes before.

To be sure there wasn't another physical reason for her stomachaches that I should treat, I had her give me a urine specimen. One rather common reason for little girls' abdominal pain is an acute urinary infection. It should always be checked out. Laura's urine was negative, which was further evidence that she had no physical reason for her pain. At this point, she certainly didn't look as if she had any more pain.

Had this been malingering on her part? Was she headed for a psychosomatic disorder? Not at all. Nearly all 4- and 5-year-old girls go through periods of stomachaches, at some time or other. Boys are much less likely to have them. Many of them are so severe that they must be differentiated from ones that need attention by just such an office visit as Laura's. As they build up in intensity, everyone's anxiety gets caught. It becomes critical that this anxiety be difused before these stomachaches become chronic. I am convinced that chronic stomachaches start out as mild ones, but are rapidly reinforced by anxiety in parents which transmits itself to the child. Stomachaches are like many other symptoms which occur commonly in normal, healthy children. Parents need assurance that they do not represent underlying pathology. They, in turn, will reassure the child. As a child runs the gamut of mild aches and pains—headaches, stomachaches, legaches—people around her easily reinforce such a symptom. It then can build up to a "real" psychosomatic phenomenon all too quickly.

It is interesting to me that I rarely see 4- or 5-year old boys with such recurring stomachaches, unless they are chronically constipated, or unless they have other reasons such as low blood sugar or urinary problems. But many girls of this age seem to have them. This sex difference has intrigued me and I have no real explanation for it. I can surmise that it is an unconscious identification with their mothers. But how many little girls know that their mothers have periodic cramps? Do mothers of girls pay more attention to their daughter's bellyaches? I know of no research to answer this.

THE WEAK LINK

Stomachaches (and a number of other symptoms) seem to come on at times of tension, fatigue, or when a new school situation is imminent. As was explained earlier, all children seem to have one weak organ. Whenever they are tired or stressed or are coming down with an illness, this organ reflects it. Some have headaches, others vomit or sleep a lot, and others, like Laura, have stomachaches. Many children have a mild sensitivity to the lactose sugar in milk. A colleague of mine, Dr. Ron Barr, when he was at Children's Hospital in Boston, found that such children occasionally developed severe stomachaches from their usual intake of milk, but only when they were upset for other reasons. Stress or fatigue set off a symptom which would otherwise be underground. Hence, a child like Laura might profit from cutting out milk at exciting or stressful periods. Some children are intolerant of other foods that bother only at times of stress. Low blood sugar can give certain children a stomachache every morning on school days; it never happens on weekends. These children are anxious about school, and this stress adds to the child's inability to deal with the lowered blood sugar. Then their intestines reflect the stress they are under. Abdominal pain is the result of stress plus the physiological condition—not one factor alone. A combination of several things—stress, excitement, and otherwise mild intolerance and a slightly vulnerable organ—can work together to produce symptoms. This additive theory helps me understand otherwise baffling symptoms.

In Laura's case, reassurance at each episode, coupled with ruling out more serious reasons for her stomachaches will eventually reduce the anxiety she and her mother would naturally have about them. I recommended to Mrs. Smith that she explain the reasons for her pain to Laura as well as she could (that they came when Laura was tired or excited), to assure her that they weren't likely to be serious. And *even if they were,* we could fix them. It has always amazed me that even small children can profit by an interpretation of their problems. A small child profits by reassurance, respect, and shared understanding.

HEADACHES

Headaches in children also are perplexing. Those that recur at regular intervals are even more so. It is rare for a child of less than four years of age to complain of a headache. Although she may have them before this, the concept of localizing the pain and of complaining about it in order to get relief is generally beyond the capabilities of a small child. There are special times of day when crankiness and other signs of disintegration are likely to be associated with headaches in preschool children. Around breakfast and in the late afternoon after a long, hard day, low blood sugar is likely to be added to fatigue. These are common times for headaches in all children, and it is likely that even small children may experience headaches during these periods, of which they are incapable of complaining.

By the ages of 4 and 5, complaints of headaches begin to surface in many children's lives. Since this is a period when children identify more closely with adults around them, one wonders whether they first get the concept by imitating an adult or older child. Other somatic symptoms, such as stomachaches, obstipation (stool withholding), and leg aches are likely to be recurrent complaints at this time as well. Many children have headaches from time to time after the ages of 6 or 7. I know of no research as to the association between the age of onset and the severity of symptoms. It is unlikely that most headaches will lead to severe ones later on.

Certain children who begin to complain of headaches in early childhood will eventually end up with migraine headaches. Since migraines have a genetic component, it is unlikely that they can be prevented by any parental efforts. As with other, milder forms of headaches, there are likely to be many triggers which set them off, rather than any one cause. Certain of these triggers may be more powerful in some children than in others. The typical migraine starts with what is called the *prodrome,* either a feeling of nausea or eye signs—such as flashes or crinkles in the visual field. Migraines are likely to occur at regular intervals, are incapacitating for as much as 24 hours, and are accompanied by malaise and anorexia. Migraine sufferers learn to dread them unless a specific antidote can be found. I would urge parents of children with regular, severe headaches to have a checkup for migraine and to try the various new medications which show some promise. Since each child is responsive to a different medication, several should be tried before giving up. *Any severe headache* which has an acute onset, lasts for more than a few hours, and is not relieved by aspirinlike substances, *deserves the attention of the child's physician* (see Guidelines at end of chapter).

I would like to address the milder form of headache which is not so severe and which disappears after rest or mild painkillers and parental attention. These are usually so mild that they do not interfere with the child's play or his activity as long as it is interesting enough. However, they are likely to surface with boredom, loneliness, fatigue, or with being reprimanded by a parent. They occur at the end of a busy day or at predictable times. They are associated with getting dressed, getting ready for school, being called to supper, being sent to bed—almost any unpleasant demand. Their timing is likely to make them easy to understand. If they are reinforced by a sympathetic parent or babysitter, they are likely to worsen and recur on a regular basis. Since they are patently triggered off by pressures on the child, and since they disappear when the pressures are replaced by sympathetic attention, parents are not likely to be too anxious about them. The developmental phase which triggered them as a symptom will pass, and they are likely to be a time-limited complaint in the middle childhood years.

Certain children, however, may develop a more severe form of headache which is not as easy for parents to understand. Since they are also likely to occur at a predictable time of day and are more incapacitating to the child, parents are likely to worry about them and wonder about their cause. The child herself will soon begin to dread them and to worry when she is developing one of these episodic headaches. If they are not as severe as true migraines and there is no genetic history for migraine, and *if* the child's physician has been consulted to rule out underlying reasons for them, the parents themselves may be able to alleviate them with the right approach. There are certain concepts which may be useful to parents in this attempt and in avoiding the factors which set up headaches as a recurring psychosomatic problem in the first place.

MULTIPLE TRIGGERS

As I suggested earlier, each child is likely to have an "Achilles heel." Every stress or impending illness will express itself in this organ. In this organ there is a lower threshold for resisting stress, and as a result, it reflects the struggles in the child's coping system. As she matures, this threshold is likely to rise, and if she has learned enough about coping with stress, she is likely to "outgrow" these symptoms. Meanwhile, it may serve a purpose as a release mechanism or by forcing an active, tense child to slow down and relax. At any rate, it is worth trying to understand the pressures or stresses which will set off such symptoms. Such insight can help parents reduce their anxieties, and help the child understand herself.

Combinations of stresses are likely to precipitate the symptoms. One stress alone may not be sufficient. From time to time, the final trigger will be a different one, so it is critical to think of many small factors which can add up to a large one.

Time of day is usually predictable, as I mentioned above. Before or after breakfast the child's metabolism is likely to be out of rhythm with the demands on her—to get up, to get dressed, to be ready for school. All of these demand interest and cooperation at a time when her body is at a low ebb. Many children store and mobilize blood sugar poorly. Although they have no real or detectable pathologic condition (such as true hypoglycemia, detectable by blood tests of sugar levels), hypersensitivity, jumpiness, slow-to-warm-up behavior, as well as headaches, are symptoms of low blood sugar. They improve when the child is given a sugar or high calorie-content meal. The headache will then subside. But it may recur later in the morning. As the body insulin rises to meet the circulating sugar, it often overshoots, and low blood sugar recurs again an hour or so after breakfast, just as school is starting. The headache which accompanies these dips in body sugar looks and acts psychosomatic. The child is branded as a malingerer, and she begins to feel like one. But the headaches are real.

I would urge parents to try a regime which has helped many such children. Place a glass of orange juice or any quickly absorbed sugar-containing drink by her bedside at night. Before she gets out of bed in the morning, she should drink it and stay quiet in bed for a few more minutes until it is absorbed. Her blood sugar level will rise and she will begin to feel better. By the time she comes to breakfast, the level will be adequate, she will have energy and feel like eating breakfast. A breakfast of long-lasting protein—such as milk, an egg, or cereal—will help to prevent the acute drop in blood sugar later in the morning which would result from simpler carbohydrates. A midmorning snack at school also will help maintain blood sugar levels. In this way the headache as well as the other symptoms of hypoglycemia may be avoided. If this regime helps alleviate symptoms, it is one that is certainly worth pursuing and is an indication that the child's blood sugar is a factor in producing her headaches.

Stress, fatigue, and impending illness are all factors which cumulatively can produce headaches in vulnerable children. It certainly helps to interpret these afterward to the child herself. As she gets older and has better control over her activity and the stresses in her life, she can understand the reasons behind the headaches and will not be as worried about herself.

Anxiety adds a strong factor to the other possible triggers. A child easily can feel that she is bad or deserves headaches if they recur often. If a child can understand that it is not her fault or a sign of badness, and if she can be helped to realize that all children are likely to have a part of the body that reflects normal stresses, even a 5- or 6-year-old will benefit. Without such an explanation, a child will learn to dread the onset of the headache, to become depressed and helpless. Even the child's self-image can begin to be impaired over time, and she may begin to feel crippled by these recurrent headaches. If this can be avoided and self-confidence and ability to ward off headaches encouraged, many children who have recurrent headaches in mid-childhood outgrow them in late childhood and adolescence.

A diary of the timing of onset of each severe headache and the events or stresses which surround it can uncover a trigger which is common to many or all of them. Since stress and fatigue can't be entirely eliminated, the parents and the child can plan to eliminate other triggering factors at a time when stress and fatigue are inevitable. As a last resort, I would urge parents to search for and provide the child with a pain reliever which works for her, then give her control over taking it early and by herself. Aspirin or an aspirin substitute (1 grain per year up to 10 grains is an adequate dose) often works. For migraine headaches, there are more specific therapies such as the exgotrates, but they have side effects and may make the child jittery, flushed, and tense, so they must only be used if there are no other simpler solutions.

I feel that the use of medication or pills is a last resort, and simpler measures such as rest or diet should be tried first. When they are necessary, however, it is important for the child to realize that she can manage them herself. The ability to decide when a painkiller is needed to conquer the impending headache can be a real reinforcement for the child's feeling of competence. Most important of all, insight into the kind of factors which lead to the headaches, coupled with an understanding that they are not a sign of weakness or inadequacy, will encourage the child to feel in control of her own body.

GUIDELINES

1. *Stomachaches.* If, even after an attempt to quiet the child, there is a localized painful area which increases over time, and if, despite an aspirinlike substance, it increases, the child's physician should be consulted. If there is generalized spasm of the abdominal muscles or pain in an area of the belly induced by indirect pressure in another area, it may be a sign of trouble. Other possible signs of obstruction are recurrent, excruciatingly sharp pain which becomes more and more localized, no bowel movements, forceful vomiting, and boardlike abdomen. A physician should check a child who exhibits any of these signs.

2. *Headaches.* When headaches increase in severity and frequency, and when they are accompanied by other signs of intracranial pressure such as difficult vision, wandering eye, nausea and vomiting, or any weakness of arms or legs, a physician should be consulted. Even if the headaches are not due to any serious problem but are severe and recur often enough, a doctor may help find some of the reasons that are contributing to them. A family history of recurring headaches may point to migraine. Migraine headaches are likely to be regular in occurrence; they usually are accompanied by other symptoms such as nausea, fatigue, or sleepiness, or eye signs such as crinkly lights which make the child's vision fuzzy. If headaches prove to be migraine in type, there are specific medications which help, and a specialist should be consulted.

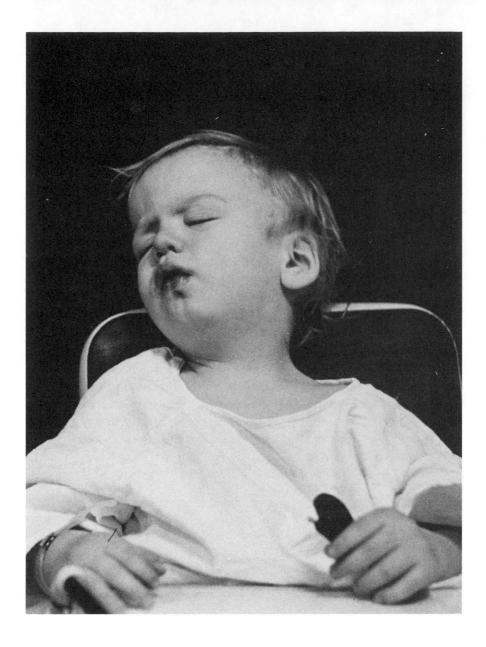

11
HANDLING CROUP, SEIZURES, AND OTHER ACUTE EMERGENCIES

There are a few emergencies which severely test parents' ability to cope and to maintain stability. As a parent, of course, one should always be ready for an emergency. But no matter how well prepared, certain kinds of illnesses and emergencies are so frightening at the time that no parent can remain totally calm. The anxiety which is created becomes a source of adrenalin for meeting the emergency. Of *course,* a parent shows how frightened he or she is, and of *course,* that anxiety in the parent adds to the child's own; but after the emergency is met, there are ways to reassure the child. Among the more frightening conditions are croup and febrile convulsions. Also, poisoning is an emergency for which all parents should be prepared.

CROUP

Croup is always frightening to parents, and yet maintaining one's cool can be really helpful to the child, for croup is made more severe by anxiety. Knowing what to do may help a parent feel calm and offer a reassuring response. Croup is a situation which parents can usually handle if they know what to look for and when to get really concerned.

The call came in the middle of the night. I heard Mrs. Kane's frantic voice: "Doctor, Jim can't breathe! He's choking to death. Can you do something, quick!"

Roused from sleep, I felt my own adrenalin begin to rise. I knew Mrs. Kane well enough to realize that she was really frightened or she wouldn't have called at this time. In addition, I had always thought of her as an unusually steady person; we'd been through crises together before, and I'd been impressed with her ability to meet them.

I asked her the questions I needed to ask to determine whether this 5-year-old boy was in such acute distress that he needed the rescue squad, or to be rushed to the hospital, or whether we could cope with his problem at home. I thought of the first two alternatives only as last resorts. Rushing him off with the rescue squad would be extremely frightening, for him as well as for his family. Taking him to the hospital emergency ward would also be frightening. To be examined by strangers, to have the painful blood tests and the X-rays which are a routine part of admission to any hospital, would produce needless anxiety, unless there were no alternatives. I would prefer going to the child's home and examining him there, for we knew each other well, he trusted me, and I knew that under those favorable circumstances his worrisome breathing symptoms would not increase.

But first, the questions: "Could he have choked on any foreign body?" I wanted to know. "Where is the breathing difficulty located?" "Does he have trouble when he breathes in, or when he breathes out?"

I ascertained from Mrs. Kane that he hadn't choked on anything and that he was frightened but not out of control or in shock. Mrs. Kane was so frantic that she couldn't answer my other questions successfully, so I asked her to put Jim up to the phone. If I could hear him breathe into the phone, I could tell where the difficulty was.

Had he been wheezing audibly, and had his wheezes taken place during the exhaling phase of his breathing, I would have diagnosed asthma or bronchitis. There are specific medications for these, and they need not be treated as emergencies unless he was in terrible distress.

Had he made crackling sounds at the end of each breath, and if his breathing had been short, shallow, and rapid, and had his fever been rising, I could have been fairly sure he was coming down with pneumonia. We could treat that with antibiotics, and it wouldn't be a real emergency.

Had his breathing been rough and gurgly, each breath accompanied by noisy snoring, I would have concluded that there was a swelling which created an obstruction in his nose or the back of his throat, and I would have concluded that he had an upper respiratory infection. Again, this would not be an emergency, and I could help them deal with it without the hospital.

But what I heard as the receiver was placed next to Jim's mouth was a raspy foghorn noise as he drew in his breath. I concluded that the obstruction—an acute inflammatory swelling—was in the area of the larynx or voice box and trachea and that he was coming down with croup. (This diagnosis was verified when his mother told me that his ribcage and the area above his breastbone sank in deeply every time he tried to draw in his breath.)

Croup almost always comes on acutely and is usually a complication of a common cold. It comes on in the middle of the night, often when the weather is about to change to rain or snow. The immediate problem is the acute obstruction that is created by inflammation and swelling around the airway. Whenever a child wakes up to find it difficult to get his breath, he will panic. As he panics, the muscles of the airway go into more spasm, and the trouble in breathing increases. If, when his parents are awakened, they in turn panic, the anxiety of the child will also worsen. My first job was to calm Jim's mother and father. If they could relax, they could help him right away by taking him into a steamy room such as the bathroom with all the hot water outlets turned on full force.

I told Mrs. Kane to do this and to take a rocking chair into the bathroom, too. If she sat in the chair, rocking Jim, he would be likely to calm down, and the steam in the room would help the spasm in his larynx to relax. I assured her that he could be successfully treated this way. (The very rare case in which the epiglottis is so swollen that it won't relax is not only unusual but one that can be recognized in time if the child's breathing doesn't improve as a result of this maneuver. In that case, hospitalization would be needed.)

I called the Kanes back 15 or 20 minutes after they took Jim into the soothing, steamy bathroom. Jim's breathing was better, his father told me, and he was falling asleep in his mother's lap. I told Mr. Kane that they should continue this maneuver and suggested that, if they had one, they could give Jim a lollipop to suck on—this would soothe his throat. The lollipop would not only be soothing but also would cheer him up and let him know he wasn't too sick. Its symbolic value would help calm him down. I pointed out that croup will always improve in the morning, then return at night, but by the second or third night, most children know that their croup can be managed; and so it is not likely to get worse because of anxiety. (If Jim had had fever with his croup and appeared to be exhausted or very sick, I would have gone to him immediately, for these are signs of infection which call for antibiotics and for more drastic treatment. In 95% of acute cases of croup, treated as Jim was being treated (often supplemented with an expectorant cough medicine), the children will respond well, especially in cases of an initial episode. There is a rare kind of croup known as acute epiglottitis, in which emergency care at a hospital can become critical. For in this rare kind, the swelling of the bulb of the epiglottis will obstruct breathing, and an operation in which a tube is inserted in the throat to let in air becomes necessary. But in most cases, if not all, this first maneuver of steam and calming is worth a real try before hospitalization becomes indicated.

When a child like Jim is admitted to the emergency ward for croup or epiglottitis, I would urge parents to be sure that one of them stays with the child at all times. If he needs to be placed in an oxygen tent with steam in order to relax the spasm, ask if you can't get into the tent, too. Being placed in a tent can be a frightening experience, and if the child is put in it alone, fright may increase respiratory distress to the point of making an otherwise unnecessary operation necessary. If a parent can be with the child in this new and strange situation, the child may not mind it.

When I called the Kanes a second time a half hour later, Jim was better. His lollipop was in his mouth, and both he and his mother were relaxed. When I saw Jim the next morning, he was slightly hoarse, but he was playing all around my office. I examined him as he cheerfully sat on my table. He croaked a little as he talked to me. I laughed, and he laughed. I said, "Jim, you were really scared last night, weren't you?" He got serious and said, "But the lollipop made me feel better." I looked seriously at him and said, "You won't need to be so scared tonight when you wake up with that crazy breathing. Mommy and I know what to do to help you. She'll buy a steamer to keep next to your bed, get you a lollipop, and you can prop yourself up on pillows in bed. You'll be okay." He took in everything I was saying with wide eyes and a serious, puckered little face. When he got worse again that night, both he and his mother followed my directions, and they worked. Keeping him out of the hospital had really paid off. He was not traumatized. The second time he was not even very frightened, and both he and his mother had learned how to cope with the croup. If it occurred again, they were prepared.

CONVULSIONS

Convulsions are another emergency for which parents need advice and preparation. They occur commonly with high fevers. They can come on even before the fever appears, as the child is developing an infection which will cause fever. He may begin to be very sick looking, may hallucinate, or seem unreachable. Finally, his whole body will stiffen, his legs and arms will straighten out in rigid tension, his eyes will roll back, and his neck will arch. The stiff phase may last a short period or a longer one (several minutes). In any event, it will seem like an eternity to the parent who is watching. Finally, the rigid phase will be followed by severe, rhythmic jerks of the extremities, of the face and mouth, and of the entire body. This is the phase in which it is conceivable that the child might bite his tongue, although this is extremely unlikely. A moderate hard, blunt object placed between the teeth will prevent any real damage. The only real danger to the child is that the convulsion can be so severe that it interferes with normal breathing. If the child has gasping respirations, they are usually adequate to maintain his color. If he doesn't and begins to turn blue around the mouth, it certainly constitutes an emergency: one must prevent damage to his brain from lack of oxygen. The usual febrile convulsion does not harm the child at all. Other than its frightening aspect, it is not as serious an emergency as it appears to be.

What can parents do? First, try to protect the child's airway. If he had had anything in his mouth, clear it out with your finger. Place something between his teeth if it looks as if he might bite his tongue. Lay him down with his head flat or lower than the rest of his body, so the blood supply to his head can be maintained. Then cool him off. A lukewarm tub of water is the most soothing and often the most effective way. Alcohol rubs and ice-water sponges certainly will cool the child down, but he may hate them—and his struggles in response to them may add to the seizure. A seizure may be prolonged by too much overreaction on the part of those around the child. Unless he is in serious shape—such as having difficulty in breathing—or unless the seizure does not subside after a few minutes, rushing him off to a hospital may be too drastic and upsetting. It can even help to prolong the seizure.

The first seizure is always terrifying. It may not upset the child, for he may not remember it. But it is traumatic for parents who must observe it. Approximately 95% of seizures in children under 4 years of age accompany a high fever and are likely to be innocuous for the child. The fever sets them off because it lowers the threshold in an immature brain to a level which allows for seizures. Most of us have such a threshold, but it takes a great deal to reach it. In small children with perfectly normal brains, without a detectable abnormality that might cause seizures, such high fevers can set one off. Dehydration added to the fevers makes a seizure even more likely. The first high fever is usually the trigger in such a child, so parents of children who have already weathered a high temperature without a seizure can usually be pretty reassured that their child will not be prone to seizures.

After the seizure is under control, the parents should seek medical advice. The doctor will check several things. I first check to see that the child's neck is supple. If he cannot bend his head forward on his chest by arching his spinal cord into a letter C, a lumbar puncture should be done to rule out meningitis or a treatable infection.

It is also important to ascertain the underlying reason for the child's fever and to treat it. For, if the fever continues, he could have another seizure. In any event, he would need an aspirinlike* substance to reduce the fever and phenobarbital to raise his threshold and to reduce the chance of a repeat seizure.

There are different ways of treating such a child after the initial emergency is over, and the decision should be made by the child's own physician. Many otherwise normal children have a single episode of seizure, and with proper preventive treatment they need never have one again. Without lowered oxygen levels to the brain, seizures do not do damage in themselves. After a second seizure, I always ask for an EEG (electroencephalogram, or brain-wave test) to rule out epilepsy or another reason for seizures. Even after the first, I ask parents to consider either a low, but continuous, dose of phenobarbital to prevent a recurrence or a discontinuous course in which the parents offered the child aspirin and phenobarbital whenever they thought a fever might be going up. After innoculations, with an acute cold, or with exposure to any disease which might cause fever, it would be worth instituting this therapeutic preventive regime. For the longer one can prevent recurrences, the harder they are to set off again. As a child grows, his threshold will rise and seizures become less and less likely. By ages 4 and 5, the danger is likely to be over for children who have had only one febrile seizure.

POISONING

Poisoning is a situation which calls upon all a parent's resources. When a child ingests a toxic substance, it is necessary to act quickly and appropriately. Since no one can keep a list of common and uncommon household poisons in his or her mind, I have urged the

---

*Since aspirin itself may be associated with Reyes' syndrome, and the research results are not in, many physicians prescribe a substitute.

parents of all small children to keep a guide to emergency first aid on hand. By the age of 8 months it is time to find one that covers the situations your baby may be likely to get into. As he learns to crawl, he will explore and find things you will never have thought of. Choking on small objects on the floor can certainly happen, and a parent should learn the maneuvers necessary for clearing out a child's airway. In cases of poisoning, I recommend that patients always have an appropriate dose of ipecac (an emetic) to make him vomit if necessary. Then, if there is a poison control center or an emergency line available for advice, write the number on your phone. If something happens, you will be too distraught to find it in the phone book. Precious time can be wasted by having to look it up. Do not rush the child off to the hospital if it takes 15 minutes or more to get there. Get advice first, for you often can stop the absorption of the toxin by giving him an emetic before going on to the hospital. The most important step to take is to be prepared in advance.

These are but a few of the frightening emergencies with which parents may be faced. More comprehensive books (such as *Should I Call the Doctor?* by Christine Nelson, M.D.* or *Child Health Encyclopedia* by Richard I. Feinbloom, M.D. and the Boston Children's Medical Center†) are useful, and every family should have such a guide and emergency phone numbers on hand.

My main thesis here is that, of *course* parents are frightened, and so are children, by these emergencies. After they are over, it is wise to discuss the fears that were raised. In such a discussion a parent is doing several things: (1) admitting to his or her own fear, which the child must have sensed; (2) allowing the child to share his fears with the parent; (3) opening the way for discussion of how to handle them in the future; and (4) giving a chance to formulate plans for any future emergency. This then can become a way of reassuring the child for the future and is an opportunity to share this episode as a natural source of anxiety for all the family. A parent should be prepared to discuss any emergency many times afterwards. Each discussion is an opportunity for the child to learn more about himself.

---

*New York: Warner, 1986.
†New York: Delacorte, 1975.

12
ASTHMA

Preventing allergic disease or treating it early are both more effective than treating it after it is established. In my practice I have long been looking for the ingredients of prevention for eczema, asthma, and chronic respiratory disease. I do as much as I can to identify the potentially allergic child, even at the risk of setting up "labels" in parents' minds. The danger of looking for possible allergies is that parents who treat a perfectly healthy child as vulnerable may impair the developing child's image or frighten her into a kind of passivity. If this can be avoided, however, there is every reason to feel that preventing allergies, or treating them from the beginning, may stop the child from feeling that she is a failure, that she is crippled, by preventing the vicious cycle of disease, depression, psychosomatic compliance. Treating allergic manifestations early and including the child in her own treatment can help her feel able to conquer such a disease for herself. The feelings of helplessness and depression in the midst of an allergic episode are the worst aspects of the disease and may well create a kind of "expectancy" for being at the mercy of it. How can we prevent this outcome in a child?

AVOIDING FEAR AND PANIC

Six-year-old Jeff was in severe distress. He was having an asthma attack. This was his second visit to my office for this kind of episode within two weeks. He was discouraged and frightened. His mother felt a sense of panic. As he pulled in air, each rib stood out and the area above his breastbone sank in with the effort. As he pushed the air out against the pressure of his lungs, which were in spasm, his wheezes racked the room. His pale, strained little face turned toward me with enormous, pleading eyes. He pushed and pulled for each breath. "Do something," he said, gasping. I prepared a syringe of adrenalin to give him, explaining that the needle would hurt for a second but that then he'd soon feel better. He nodded as if to say, "Just get on with it." He barely winced as I gave him the shot. I made him lie down on my examining table, for I knew his heart would race and that he might feel dizzy after the adrenalin. He complied all too easily, turning his head away so I couldn't see how frightened he was. Within ten minutes he was getting better. His face was already flushed and fuller. His eyes were less strained, and his breathing was beginning to relax with strikingly easier respirations. After 15 minutes, he began to smile up at me.

"How do you feel?" I asked. "Already better," he gasped. I said, "See, Jeff, we do know what to do when you get your asthma attacks, don't we?" He nodded gratefully.

"But we've got to find a way for you to beat these attacks before you get this bad. This trouble you have breathing must scare you!" I pressed him. "I know, Dr. B., 'cause you told me what to do last time. But I forgot. Anyway, I didn't think it would happen again." He admitted, "I slept with my cat, and you told me not to when I had a cold."

His feeling of guilt and the reference to the hope that it would never happen again are two of the inevitable thought processes that accompany this disease—in children as well as in the adults around them. The third feeling they all have is panic—a panic that the child won't be able to get a breath and that she'll never escape this frightening condition.

Jeff's feeling of helplessness as he exerts all his energy in trying to breathe can lead to overwhelming fear. In fact, I suspect that a chld begins quickly to live in dread of "the next time" after only one or two bad bouts of such wheezing. Jeff had been wheezing badly for twelve hours before his desperate parents brought him in to see me.

By the time I began to talk to his parents about him, Jeff had hoisted his sturdy little frame off my table, had scrambled down to the floor, and was playing almost hysterically with my toys. He threw them around noisily. Watching him without a knowledge of his history, one would have thought him almost hyperactive. But he was working out the anxiety he'd just been through. As we talked, he listened to us very carefully. Even at the age of 6, this child was as concerned about himself as we were.

THE IMPORTANCE OF PREVENTION

In my 30 years of practice, I have followed an aggressive program for preventing allergies rather than only trying to treat them after they are instituted. As a result of the many asthmatic children I've cared for, only one was sick enough to require extended or frequent hospitalization. The others were able to manage their disease without using the hospital. As for eczema, I have had no severe cases; we were at least able to control the disease if we started soon enough.

Avoiding the severe, frightening aspects of these two diseases is very important to the future well-being of a child. Today we have so many more ways of helping these patients that a concerted effort from the beginning pays off. Unless we can find treatment that *works,* children begin to enter a vicious cycle of anxiety, fear, and helplessness. It is at this point that the psychosomatic aspects of the disease are laid down. Children quickly begin to feel all the hopelessness and guilt that Jeff expressed. The undermined self-image this brings about seems to me the most devastating aspect of allergic diseases.

Although such diseases as asthma can become overlaid with anxiety and may well become partly "psychosomatic" after a few frightening episodes, I do not think that asthma or eczema begin because of problems in the child or underlying family difficulties. There is likely to be a genetic predisposition which is reinforced by environmental allergens. Then, as the disese manifests itself, of *course* the sufferer gets frightened and involved with it. Asthmatic children are likely to demonstrate their anxiety to their parents and are prone to "use" the symptom for all kinds of manipulative reasons—such as rebellion, fatigue, provocation, or simply to get attention. Parents will be drawn into it inevitably as their own anxiety mounts if they are unable to control it. Their guilt, their anger, their anxiety will heighten tensions in the family and in their relationship with the child. In this way it can become all too easily a psychosomatic focus for the child and the family.

It needn't be allowed to go this far. Prevention is the best cure, but early intervention is also very effective.

In Jeff's case we had started laying the groundwork for prevention in his early infancy. We knew that there were allergies in both sides of his family. The genetic component in allergies is well known.* This inherited predisposition is then reinforced by challenges with specific allergens, which makes the disease manifest itself and sets off the cycle of recurrence.

When Jeff was a tiny infant, his father told me that he himself had been allergic to milk and had had severe eczema as a baby. Jeff's mother's brother had had asthma as a child. We talked at that time about some of the ways to avoid the possibility of allergies in infancy in their children. There is good reason to avoid triggering diseases as long as possible. They are harder to set off as a child gets older; the threshold rises over time. I am convinced that the longer an allergic manifestation can be avoided, the more difficult it will be to set it off. By the same token, the more successfully it is treated if it does occur, the better the outcome will be. In babies an allergy to cow's milk or to other foods may not express itself at the time of the challenge but will show up later, after the allergic process has been firmly set. Eczema, gastrointestinal symptoms (spitting up, diarrhea, or even "colic"), or respiratory difficulties (such as a chronically running nose) may show up weeks or months after the infant has been started on milk. If she is less than 9 months old, a wheat or egg allergy may come out as a full-blown reaction only a week or ten days after the first exposure. Meanwhile, the allergic process is getting set in place. To avoid this, I urge parents of a baby with a family history of allergies to avoid any potential allergens until the baby is older—old enough to show a direct allergic symptom.

I had urged Jeff's mother, Mrs. Scott, to breastfeed Jeff as long as she could. I instructed her to use soybean formulas as a substitute for any milk supplement in his first few months. Thus we did not challenge him with the cow's milk his father had been sensitive to. I encouraged the Scotts to wait until Jeff was 5 months old before starting him on solid foods for fear of his being allergic to them. Then they fed him only one new food at a time, waiting at least a week before trying another. If he became upset or developed a rash after a new food, they stopped it to try another. They never mixed cow's milk with his cereal, and they were careful to read the labels on baby

---

*Pediatrics, December 1981.

food jars to eliminate any possibility of feeding him mixtures of foods. Any one of these might have triggered his allergic tendencies. They waited to try wheat until he was 7 months old and postponed egg yolk until he was over 9 months. He broke out with hives the day he ate egg yolk. After that his parents avoided eggs and custard until he was well over a year. As a result, Jeff made it through infancy without any serious skin rashes or eczema.

Mrs. Scott had been able to breastfeed him for 11 months, and we all felt this provided a tremendous protection from a cow's milk allergy. After a year Jeff had been able to start drinking cow's milk and to eat foods containing milk. We never knew whether he would have been allergic to them earlier, but this was not important. It was not easy for the Scotts to avoid these foods, and I also was concerned that my emphasis on the potential of a food allergy made them more conscious of Jeff as a vulnerable child, but the alternative was to risk the horrors of eczema or of food sensitivities. This regime is one I recommend to all parents who have an allergic family background.

Jeff grew into a vital, sturdy toddler. He fed himself by the time he was a year old, and like any other determined toddler, he insisted on trying every food on the table. By this age he was safe from reactions except for a few foods known to be allergenic: eggs, chocolate, tomatoes, and fish. The Scotts had to avoid eating these when Jeff was around so he wouldn't want to try them.

ASTHMA AND COLDS

As he grew, Jeff became more and more active. He was athletically built, and he loved to climb and to get himself into all sorts of predicaments. He was the center of any available group of active children. In spite of being the center of his family and somewhat overindulged at home, he was so charming and thoughtful with other children that he was every child's favorite in his class. Jeff was rarely ill in his first three years. Two colds ended with prolonged runny noses. Only one ended with an earache and needed to be treated with antibiotics. He seemed not to be particularly vulnerable to respiratory infections through these first years. Many allergic children not only get everything they come into contact with; each upper respiratory infection hangs on so long that one runs into the other. Such children, as a result, are likely to have noses that are chronically dripping and adenoid tissue builds up; they are more likely to have internal ear and sinus complications from the blockage of too much overgrown tissue in their adenoid areas; they are liable to be snorers. (Many snoring children prove to be allergic.)

When Jeff was 3-1/2, a baby sister was born. On the surface he seemed to handle her arrival with bravado and with a certain amount of guarded tenderness. He kept insisting that she grow up to be a boy "like him," so he could play with "him," but otherwise he took her in his stride. Soon after Alison arrived, however, Jeff came down with a lingering cold and a cough. At the time it seemed as if it were a coincidence. He remained congested and somewhat wheezy at night for the next six weeks. We tried antihistamines to dry him up, and they helped some, but it took him a long time to overcome this infection.

A few months later, at the time of his fourth birthday, and on two more occasions in the next year, Jeff had long drawn-out upper respiratory infections. After two of these, I urged his parents to try to remove allergens from his room. We talked about eliminating simple things, such as the feather pillow and stuffed animals from his bed, and covering the horsehair mattress with a plastic envelope. I tried to explain to them that, in light of the family history, it might be that his colds were prolonged by a mild form of allergic congestions which lasted after the infection had been conquered. They assured me that he could not be allergic to any of the things I wanted them to remove, for he'd been living with them all along without any trouble. I told them that the manifestation of an allergy in the form of asthma, eczema, or even chronically running noses can be a cumulative process, like building a block tower. You can have many little blocks sitting on each other for years without toppling. A child can sleep on horsehair and feathers (both of which are common allergens) for years. But if you add on too many blocks, or add on a big one, such as an acute respiratory infection or exposure to a special allergen for that child (cats are a typical example), or even an emotional stress, the block tower will topple. In Jeff's case respiratory disease seemed to be the trigger. As we talked, I could sense that the Scotts were resistant to accepting my suggestions. I didn't press them, for Jeff's stuffiness was not debilitating at the time, and the antihistamines we gave him were helping. In retrospect, however, I do wonder whether they might have avoided some of Jeff's trouble had they acted early.

When he began to snore at night, I began to press his parents harder. His snoring was a symptom of a buildup of adenoid tissue. I felt that his long, drawn out congestion was the reason for this buildup. He was paler and more washed out than he had been, and he was getting more depressed than I'd ever seen him. I was afraid that he was beginning to see himself as an invalid.

Again we went over the elimination of the likely allergens in his room and bed, with the knowledge that half of his 24 hours was spent there. It seemed easy to substitute a synthetic pillow, to cover his mattress with a plastic envelope, and to remove stuffed animals (or restuff them with foam rubber). I urged them to remove dust-catching rugs and to lay the dust in his room by using an oil mop for his floor twice a week and to cover the outlet in his room for the hot-air furnace with a filter made of several layers of cheesecloth. I explained that no single one of these things would necessarily make a dramatic difference in his congestion, but that they might eliminate some of the small blocks in the tower he was building up. I found out then that he'd been sleeping with the cat in his bed since his sister came—as a compensation for her arrival. All of us groaned at the possibility of taking the cat away from him. But I warned them that she might be a large factor in his difficulty. Cats and other fur-bearing animals are highly allergenic—both because of their own fur and because they carry dust and molds in the fur. Most children are allergic to furry animals if they are allergic at all. The Scotts resisted separating Jeff and the cat, so I recommended that they start with a simple cleanup to see whether that would help. It may be a nuisance to maintain a relatively dust-free environment, but it can certainly help in keeping respiratory disease at a minimum. In the polluted atmosphere of a city today, there are many circulating respiratory irritants that cannot be eliminated, but those around a child's room and bed can be.

Jeff did improve a bit after this cleanup, and we were all grateful. The cat did not have to be removed. His snoring improved as we administered antihistamines to him, and his night cough finally disappeared. Jeff's outgoing, happy attitude returned. He literally bounced out of my office in the spring. We all hoped we were done with his respiratory problems.

In early October he was back in my office with a severe cold. This time he was wheezing as he breathed. He had to pull hard to get his breath in and had to push hard to get it out. He said, "I can't run," as if this were indeed a frightening handicap for him. His parents and I faced the possibility that this wheezing might represent a mild form of asthma which was now being added onto his acute respiratory infections. We used a double "treatment"—an antispasmodic for his wheezing and an antibiotic for the underlying infection. In general, I use antibiotic medications as little as possible, for I feel that the best thing we can do for most children is to let them build up their own immunity to infections. Antibiotics interfere with this natural process. But in an allergic child, the allergies interact with the infection, and each makes the other act in a more potent fashion. One must treat both the infection and the allergy at the same time. For most allergic children an infection is a major problem and acts as a big building block. It is likely to trigger off an asthmatic attack and is much harder for an allergic child to conquer without extra help.

On this visit I sat down with Jeff and his mother to urge them to more drastic action at home. This pattern of increasing allergic responses to each cold suggested that he might be getting asthma as a complication of each upper respiratory infection. I went over with them the cleaning up procedures. I now urged them strongly to re-move the cat and to let him decide what kind of nonallergic toy or lovey he wanted as a substitute. I reiterated my theories about the block tower and the big block of infection as an added stress. I warned them about the danger of setting up such a recurrent, chronic allergic response in his chest. I hoped that they had listened and would con-form to my suggestions. I do not always refer a child to an allergist at this point, for I know the allergist will recommend just what I have suggested to them. If the family does not listen to me, I use the allergist as an expert to add pressure to their decision making. This is the critical time to take allergic reactions seriously.

INCLUDING THE ASTHMATIC CHILD IN PREVENTION AND TREATMENT

For the first time, I felt the Scotts were really paying attention. As I questioned them, I realized that they hadn't taken my previous sug-gestions seriously. I spoke to Jeff as I talked, for I felt it was just as critical that he understand what we were doing and why. As I finished, I reminded Jeff that we had medicine that would stop his wheezing if he started it early enough in his colds. He watched me intently as I told him about it. I wanted him to feel that he could be in control. I urged him to call me himself if he had any more trouble. He was now watching me seriously and listening to me as I talked. I was pretty sure he had taken it in.

The medicine worked to control this episode. As it tapered off, Jeff called to tell me on the phone that he was better. I got him to breathe for me into the phone. I could hear no wheeze, and I told him so. He said gaily, "We fixed it. We got my bed all new, and my room's clean, Dr. B!" The joy and elation in his voice was great to hear. It was as if he had done it all himself and felt a real sense of mastery. He has had several colds since. Mild wheezing nearly always followed on the second or third day. Each time, his parents called, and we reviewed the regime of medication. We talked about when to get worried enough to call me back. I felt this relieved their anxiety to a certain extent. Then I asked to talk to Jeff so I could go over the same things with him.

The best weapon against the psychological side of this disease is to include the child in prevention. In this way she can begin to understand and control her own disease. If she should have a more severe reaction, she can be included in the therapy then as well. As she improves, she can feel that we know what to do to help.

In time Jeff will gain mastery over his disease and the fears and the feelings of guilt and helplessness will no longer complicate the situation. Jeff and his parents and I will become more and more certain that we can face up to and conquer his allergies.

It becomes even more critical that allergies in a child approaching adolescence be controlled as well as possible. I have found in my practice that a child whose allergic disease has never been too chronic or too intractable is more likely to "outgrow" allergies in adolescence. Many children who have had these tendencies in preadolescence no longer respond with allergic chests or congested upper airways as they mature. This becomes a goal well worth working for.

When these home remedies do not work, it is time for an allergic child to have the more detailed workup of an allergist. Skin testing and sensitization to specific allergens work for some children, not for others. Routine use of aminophyllinelike substances is a preventive for a certain other group. Inhalant therapy can certainly help in acute episodes, and there are new developments in the area of immunology which may help such children. The field of allergy is a fruitful one and a referral for help need not be a sign of failure. I recommend that the family, the pediatric caregiver, and especially the child be included in the allergist's recommendations. The child's feeling of being a part of her own therapy will be critical in mastering the disease. That goal is worth every effort.

GUIDELINES

1. In allergic families, avoid allergenic foods from the first. For example, if either parent has had a milk allergy in childhood, don't use milk formulas for the baby until she's 6 months old.

Breastfeeding is the safest. Next, soybean substitutes are adequate coverage for the baby's requirements. After six months, if milk is given, she will show a reaction to it and the milk formula can be discontinued.

2. Solid foods should not be started until 5 months. Each new food should be started separately—at least a week apart—so that a reaction (such as vomiting, diarrhea, or skin rash) could warn you about the baby's sensitivity to the particular food. Then that food should be discontinued.

3. Common allergens—such as dust, molds, grasses, pollens, animal hair or fur, toys or animals stuffed with kapok or feathers, feather pillows, wool blankets, hair mattresses—should be eliminated from the baby's bed. They may play an additive role in setting off an allergic reaction.

4. In small children, respiratory infections that last longer than a week or which cause wheezing or unusual congestion should warn parents that allergies may be playing a synergistic role in perpetuating the infectious process. A vigorous and preventive approach to each upper respiratory infection would be wise.

5. Asthmatic wheezing should be treated vigorously—with allergic cleanup of her environment, with medications that work. Antibiotics may be necessary for the infection, but anti-allergic medication is certainly indicated. The use of it should be explained to the child, and after she improves, she can be reminded that the medication worked. Reinforcing her awareness that "we know what to do" when she's ill will give her a feeling of mastery to help to combat the natural panic that is likely to accompany wheezing.

6. When an asthmatic attack does not respond to home medications, it is important to treat her with adrenalin or aminophyllin before the attack lasts for too long. For one thing, it is easier to break the vicious cycle of wheezing and panic if one starts treatment early. It is tremendously reassuring to a child to know that the people around her know how to make her better.

7. Including the child by explaining what is happening and how to treat it can also give her a sense of mastery. Parents must handle their own panic so that they don't reinforce it in the child. This may be the first and most difficult step.

8. When home and office medications aren't working, it is time to consult an allergist who can sort out etiological factors and recommend treatment to fit the disease. One of the most critical aspects of allergic diseases in childhood is to treat early and to

prevent chronicity of the disease and the feeling of powerlessness in the child. A feeling of mastery is the crucial antidote to the psychosomatic aspects of allergies.

9. If allergies can be controlled for a period, the chance of recurrence and of intractable buildup is reduced over time. Adolescence can be a real turning point, and many children become free of allergies as adolescent changes come about. Having this possibility in mind may help parents and child to maintain an optimistic and positive attitude.

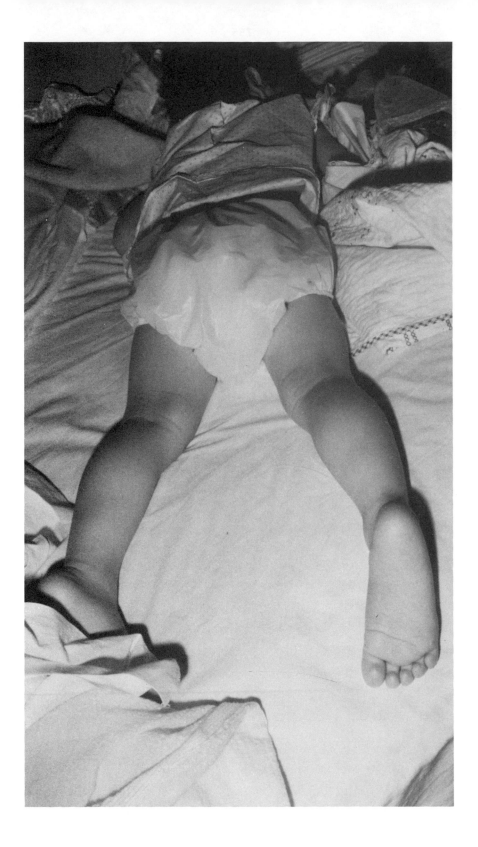

13
BEDWETTING: WHOSE SUCCESS IS IT?

"When should I worry about Bob's bedwetting? He never seems to pay any attention to his wet beds. If I talk about them, he changes the subject and I know he is either embarrassed or he wants to forget them. Either way, I am afraid that what I do will add to it as a problem. And yet, at the age of 5, I should think he would want to be dry at night. All his friends are. Have I already done something wrong? I worry about him a lot, and he knows it."

In this conversation a concerned mother has condensed the kinds of pressure which burden little boys when they have not achieved success in staying dry at night. Our society has chosen the age of 5 as an arbitrary cutoff point, after which bedwetting is defined as a "problem." In many children's clinics, this bedwetting (*enuresis*) is one of the most common reasons parents bring their preschool boys for an evaluation. Parental concern begins to peak after the age of 5 years old in our society, and yet many little boys are still wetting the bed. As Mrs. Latham said in the paragraph above, should she be worried? Was she adding to his problem if she was? The answer to the latter is yes. As for the first question, she was already worried, and Bob already knew it. His attempts to deal with her anxiety and his own by changing the subject or by not paying attention are the rather valiant efforts of a 5-year-old to handle his own feelings of failure around this issue. Of course it is sad that a 5-year-old must already see himself as a failure because of such a problem. I have had little boys in my office who have asked me pleadingly, "Will I ever be able to do it?" "Doing it" meant staying dry at night. A feeling of hopelessness clouded their eyes as they looked to me for help. My heart ached for each of these boys.

Girls appear to be more easily toilet trained in our society, and bedwetting is almost exclusively a male problem. Daytime training is much more easily achieved by both girls and boys than is control over their bladders at night. Little girls, however, trained themselves in the daytime 2.46 months earlier and were trained at night with much more ease, judging by a long-term study I carried out in 1961. In any national survey there are far fewer girls than boys who wet their beds at night. Girls who do wet are likely to have physical causes—such as bladder infection or an organically weak bladder control. Any 6-year-old girl who is still enuretic should be carefully checked for these difficulties.

SOURCES OF PRESSURE

There are many reasons for this difference between the sexes. Girls are likely to be more organized and do get day trained more easily than do boys. At the same time, we still put more pressures on boys to succeed in all areas than we do for girls. There is a heightened value placed on their success. A bed-wetting girl is not as frightening for parents or for peers as is a boy. In the eyes of society being successfully dry is symbolically equated with future success as a male. This may seem hard to believe, but it certainly seems true in my experience. Of course this unspoken pressure reinforces the psycho-somatic aspect of the problem. As a result, boys have a different experience in developing training habits. Many boys who have achieved control over their daytime toilet habits remain unable to stay dry at night for a significant period. Parents report that they "sleep too deeply" or they have "small bladders," or they "don't care." These are justifications for the most part, but they point to the nature of the difficulties which boys face.

The first two can be true as contributing factors. The latter is not likely to be an accurate appraisal of the child's reaction. So clear is our society in its expectations that by 5 years of age any small boy who still wets his bed will have gotten a message of failure. Even if his parents protect him, he will feel ashamed with his own age group. At 4 years of age nursery-school peer pressure begins. Four-year-olds who are working hard to achieve their own success are self-conscious, and it is inevitable that they will compare notes with each other. "I am dry. Are you?" "My mommy says I only wet once a week at night." "Is your bed bed *still* wet? Mine's not!" These are familiar comparisons in a 4-year-old setting. Peer pressure to be clean and dry is already mounting.

After the age of 5, a child clearly senses the concern of adults around him and begins to "hide" his defect. If he is successful, his parents are the only ones who are privy to his failure. But he must refuse to visit any of his friends overnight. He must dread a visit to grandparents lest they, too, scorn him. He must begin to prove himself in other ways. His feelings about himself as able to compete in sports, in school, and with his peer group are bound to be clouded by this symptom. As a parent, one would like to help him ignore such pressure or to mitigate it for him. Mrs. Latham's statement reflects her understanding of this danger; she wants to help Bob before this affects his entire adjustment. As he played in my office while we talked, he became alternately worried looking or "macho" in loud, aggressive play as we talked about his wet beds. His mother and I suddenly realized that we should have discussed this privately, although I often find that a child senses that he is being discussed behind the closed door of my office and becomes just as anxious. For this reason I usually ask a parent to call me in the morning call hour on the day of the office visit so we can discuss it without his presence. I can be alerted to the issues, size them up, and if it thus seems wise to discuss any of them with him, I can make the choice while he is there. Discussing it in front of him can be a help if one can use the discussion to encourage him to express his feelings and to feel less sense of failure. But if his defenses are too strong and his anxiety about himself is already too fixed, this may not work. I couldn't tell about Bob until I examined him. When I started to examine him, he was patently anxious. As I listened to his heart, palpated his abdomen, he demonstrated concern: "Am I okay?" When I tried to pull down his pants to examine his penis, he fell completely apart. He whimpered and cried. He grabbed for his underwear. He crossed his legs to keep me from prying. He always had been easy with me before. Now he was showing me how vulnerable he felt. He was telling me clearly that he knew he was "bad" or "defective."

What a cruel pressure for a child of only 5! How has it arisen in a caring, concerned family? Mrs. Latham already feels the same sense of failure that Bob does. Their feelings are bound to reinforce each other unconsciously, no matter how hard they try to deny them on the surface. When indeed should she take it seriously as a source of failure in his development? When should she have him evaluated for physical or psychological defects which might be contributing to this failure? And how can she reassure him about himself?

Dr. Ronald MacKeith of London wrote a monograph in 1973 about some physiological aspects of this problem of bedwetting.* He was convinced that there were many children whose bladders were small and remained immature for years, long after the ones who found control easily. These boys (they were rarely girls) needed to urinate more frequently day and night. To help them achieve nighttime control, he recommended that during the day they try to hold onto urine for increasingly longer periods so that they would "stretch their bladders" and learn to control their sphincters while they were awake and conscious. This conscious control could be transferred to hours of sleep. This worked for some but not for many of them. There were still an enormous number for whom any physical immaturity was overshadowed by the psychological feelings of failure they had developed. This daytime control did not transfer to the night. Unfortunately for such children, we haven't even any successful techniques which might define how much of their problem is physical. X-rays do not help enough, and there are no other tests thus far which can categorize these children as immature physically. By the time they are classified as enuretic, they are likely to see themselves as failures.

BASIC TOILET TRAINING

My own approach to this problem in my pediatric practice has been to try to *prevent* this sense of failure. A regime which I have recommended with parents has proven successful with thousands of children. A good start in early toilet training can help avoid later problems.† At some time after the child is 18 months of age, a "potty chair" on the floor is introduced as the child's "own chair." Association between it and the parents' toilet seat is made verbally. At some routine time, the mother takes him each day to sit on his chair in all his clothes. Otherwise, the unfamiliar feeling of a cold seat can interfere with any further cooperation. At this time she sits with him, reads to

---

*Kelvin, I., MacKeith, R.C., and Meadow, S.R., "Bladder Control and Enuresis." *Spastics International* Mono, Nos. 48, 49, 1973

†See Brooks, J.S., and the staff of the Boston Children's Medical Center, *No More Diapers!* (New York: Delacorte Press, 1971). Also see Brazelton, T.B., *Doctor and Child* (New York: Delacorte Press, 1976).

him, or gives him a cookie. Since he is sitting on a chair on the floor, he is free to leave at will. There should never be any coercion or pressure to remain.

After a week or more of his cooperation in this part of the venture, he can be taken for another period with his diapers off to sit on the chair in the same routine. Still no attempt to "catch" his stool or urine is made. "Catching" his stool at this point can frighten him and result in his "holding back" for a longer period thereafter. This gradual introduction of the routine is made to avoid setting up fears of strangeness and of loss of part of himself.

When his interest in these steps is achieved, he can be taken to his pot a second time during the day. This can be after his diapers are soiled, to change him on the seat, dropping his dirty diaper under him into the pot and pointing out to him that this is the eventual function of his chair.

When some understanding and the wish to comply coincide, the child will one day use the pot on a routine trip. Then he can be taken several times a day to "catch" his urine or stool, providing he remains willing.

As interest in performance grows, the next major step becomes feasible. All diapers and pants are removed for short periods, the toilet chair is placed in his room or play area, and his ability to perform by himself is pointed out. He is encouraged to go to his own pot when he wishes and by himself. He may be reminded periodically. When he is ready to perform alone, this becomes an exciting accomplishment, and many children take over the function entirely at this point. Training pants can be introduced, the child instructed as to their removal, and they can help bring about autonomous control. The excitement which accompanies mastering these steps by himself makes it well worth postponing them until this is possible.

Teaching a boy to stand for urination is an added incentive. It helps him identify with his father, with other boys, and is often an outlet for a normal amount of exhibitionism. Standing to urinate is most easily learned by watching and imitating other male figures. It is better to introduce this after bowel training is complete. Otherwise, the boy may try standing for all functions.

Nap and night training are best left until well after the child shows an interest in staying clean and dry during the day. This may be one to two years later, but often it happens coincidentally with daytime achievement. When the child shows an interest in night training, the parent can offer to help by waking him in the early evening and offering him a chance to go to the toilet. A pot painted with luminous paint by his bedside is often a useful "gimmick." He is reminded that this is there for early morning use also. Some children who are eager and ready to remain dry at night have needed further help from the parents to awake in the early morning. When this is not forthcoming, they fail in their efforts at night, lose interest, and feel guilty in their failure. Then enuresis and "giving up" may follow.

Success is applauded as the child's achievement, but when there is a breakdown, the parent is urged to stop the process and to reassure the child. He needs the reassurance that he is not "bad" in his failure to achieve and that everything will work out when he is "ready." When I examined the records of the group of children who followed the regime I suggested, I found that the incidence of failures (as defined by enuresis, chronic constipation, and such "psychosomatic" symptoms in the bowel or urine areas that could be influenced by toilet training practices) was only 1.4%. This is very low compared to the available statistics from surveys in the United States and Europe. In the United States, where pressured toilet training has not been as prevalent, enuresis is said to be likely to occur in 5–8% of boys. In England in 1965, figures as high as 15% were found. English authors maintain that this difference has to do with early and pressured toilet training of children, with parents starting to press children during the first year. Our society has learned to wait until the second year and to try to elicit the child's own interest and cooperation.

I am sure now that success in the toilet area should be the child's own autonomous achievement, not success by the parent in choosing the right technique to "train" him. Unless he feels it is something he wants to achieve, parental efforts will always be seen as pressure. On the other hand, when a regimen can be worked out for capturing the interest of the child and his developing independence, the excitement of achieving success becomes a powerful additional force for the child. In *Doctor and Child* I urged parents to examine their own feelings of pressure from society to toilet train the child early.

In deciding whether the child is ready, parents can look for the following: (1) the desire to imitate and identify with others (ages 1-1/2–2 years); (2) the sense of controlling and making choices about where and when to dispose of important parts of oneself (such as urine and bowel movements) that comes with the concept of the permanance of important persons and objects (by the end of the second year); (3) the developing sense of orderliness and where things belong (age 2); (4) motor skills to walk to and away from the toilet (18–24 months); (5) the beginning of control over negativism and the autonomy which comes with that (end of second year); (6) awareness of peers and their achievements in this area (2–3 years); and (7) the ability to speak about and to conceptualize the complex messages which are necessary in this area—of feeling the need for urination or defecation, holding on to get to a special place designated for such functions by society (3–5 years). The child will be maturing in all these ways by the end of the second year. Before that, any training must be imposed by others, and will not be the child's own initiative.

LETTING A CHILD TAKE OVER

Parents in the United States now are certainly more aware of the importance of fostering the child's interest and cooperation than they were. In the 30 years since I started in practice, the incidence of failure has decreased dramatically, and it seems to me to prove the value of a child-oriented approach. But there are still pressures on parents. Some experts offer advice about "training a 2-year-old child in 24 hours" or a program of negative reinforcement using an alarm or a signalling device in a child's bed which sets off when he wets—or a positive reinforcement system in which the child is given a cookie, candy, or a gold star when he achieves success. These are all parent-oriented programs and imply that it is up to parents to see that the child is successful. Failure in any or all of these will imply that both the parent and the child are failures. Also, since the implication of such programs is that they work for everyone else, the families who "fail" feel even more deficient and isolated.

I would urge all parents to evaluate their goals in this area of toileting before the child is 18 months old. If they can see the goal as the child's own success rather than theirs, they can work to divert their own involvement. When our fourth child, a boy, was 6 years old, he was still wetting his bed. I was personally affronted. I felt like a failure as a parent, and I foresaw a damaged self-image for his future. By way of protecting him but of subtly letting him know how I felt, I helped him change his wet sheets each morning. One day this reticent 6-year-old said to me, "Dad, why are you so upset about my bedwetting?" I fairly snorted, "I'm *not!*" He rejoined, "Yes, you are." He didn't add, as he might have, "But you needn't be." I never spoke of this again. I stopped "helping" him, and within a week he was dry at night. He'd demonstrated to me what I'd preached to others for years, that I'd made it *my* problem instead of *his.*

When successes are achieved by the child, they should certainly be acknowledged, but overemphasis can reinforce them out of proportion to their value to the child. In other words, can you read the child's feelings about success or failure? Can you manage to see it his way rather than yours or society's? I realize that this is a difficult assignment, for each child is different, and there are no universal guidelines. But a child whose maturation in this area—either physical or psychological—is slower than others around him may need support. He may need to see himself as developing more slowly—but surely. In any area it is difficult to be slower than one's peers. But understanding that one can be slow but can eventually catch up is surprisingly reassuring. A child instinctively feels that failure in an area is equivalent to being "bad." Reassurance that it's different and even difficult, but not bad, can be an important message. It is important to help the child who wets his bed realize that in his case achievement may be likely to take longer and that each child needs his own timing.

Praising a boy's maturation and achievement in other areas of his development may be an indirect but important way of giving him support. As in a lot of the problems we've discussed, efforts to give a boy special time to identify with his father, a girl with her mother, and each with the other parent may be a lot more to the point than any effort directed at the symptom itself.

GUIDELINES

If and when the child indicates that he wants help in staying dry at night, there are a few measures which might help. They are not likely to be magically successful and should not be approached as if the entire ballgame was to be won or lost by utilizing them.

1. Parents can wake a child to urinate before they go to bed. He must get himself up to go. It is of no value to take him half asleep to empty his bladder. If he is willing to go by himself, he may learn to wake up by himself. He then can be reminded that early morning is another time to try to wake up. An alarm clock or radio may be of help, although I've rarely seen this work. When he is ready to wake up for a full bladder, he'll break through his own deep sleep pattern.

2. A special trip with his father to buy a pot for the side of the bed can be a symbol of his father's support in this difficult step. Luminous paint which will light up at night can be painted on by them as a "team." When his father rouses him at night, he

can use this special pot by his bedside so he won't have so far to go to the bathroom. However, this must *not* become another source of pressure.

3. Subtle efforts are needed to keep him from feeling too guilty—such as keeping him in diapers until he's really ready to stay dry. It's embarrassing to have soaked the whole bed unwittingly.

4. When he wants to discuss it, a parent can talk to him about his individual development, the pressures on him and the problems in the maturation of his bladder which may be interfering with success in this area. If this is a real dialogue, the discussion may be tremendously reassuring to him. Your attitude and tone can express lack of anxiety. Such a discussion may reassure a child who is all too ready to compare himself to his more successful peers.

5. All of us need to reevaluate the "magical" cutoff point of 5 or 6 years. This becomes the source of society's pressure on children who may have either physical or psychological reasons for being slower to mature—and of even more pressure on the parents. We must be careful not to define success or failure in the child's development in a way that may affect him and his future. A symptom of bedwetting should not be allowed to make a child feel like a failure in society, when it could become an occasion for accomplishment and pride.

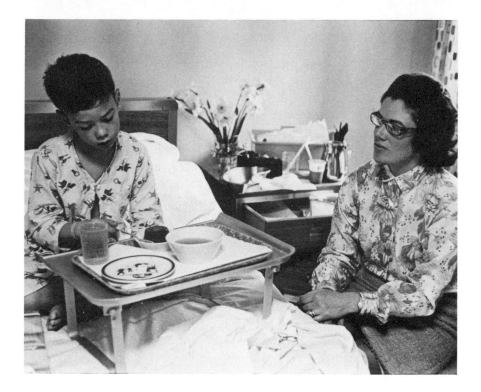

14
LISTENING TO THE HOSPITALIZED CHILD

"Tommy has to have his adenoids out next week. He's scared and I'm scared. How do I prepare him—or should I? Should I try to stay with him? What can I expect from him when he comes home? Will he be angry with me, and hard to cope with? I want to cry when I even think about it!"

Mrs. Landis was an earnest, capable young mother who wanted to do the best she could by her children. Tommy was a 5-year-old who had had so many earaches and prolonged sieges with infected tonsils and adenoids that we all were desperate. He had spent the winter on antibiotics, being treated for ear infections which wouldn't clear up. By now he was washed out-looking, pale, and exhausted. He could no longer breathe through his nose because of the enlarged adenoids, and his snoring at night rocked the household. He could barely hear when he was spoken to. Now he sat quietly in the chair across the room, resigned to being sick and to missing most of the conversation around him. He was a pitiful copy of the vigorous, playful child he had been last year. Despite our attempts to avoid an operation it looked now as if nothing else would do but to remove the huge adenoids which obstructed his breathing and were blocking the internal ducts to his ears. His desperate parents were ready to do anything to prevent a repetition of the winter we'd just been through. Even Tommy seemed to look forward to the time when he would feel

167

well again and he, too, seemed to understand that there was nothing else to do but to resort to an operation. His quiet passivity seemed to represent the patience of a much older person who was resigned to waiting for relief—of *any* kind.

MAKING HOSPITALIZATION A POSITIVE EXPERIENCE

Mrs. Landis' questions were those of an intelligent, caring mother who was preparing herself as well as her child for the impending trauma which a hospitalization represented. Thanks to such vocal leaders in England as John Bowlby and the Robertsons, we all are well aware of the potentially traumatic effects on a developing child's emotional life a hospitalization can wreak. Separation from home and parents, and the attendant pain and illness are all potential insults to the child's development. In the past few years childrens' hospitals have begun to change drastically—to include parents on the wards, to plan more active programs for children in the area of their emotional needs and which attempt to alleviate the potential psychological effect of illness and separation from home. Organizations of parents, such as the one which calls itself Parents Concerned for Hospitalized Children*, or another, Children in Hospitals†, have formed to press for changes in hospital procedures in order to treat the total child and her reactions to being ill and hospitalized rather than just treating her disease, as we had in the past.

Implicit in Mrs. Landis' questions was a belief that if she did the right things, she could soften the blow for Tommy. I heartily agreed with her and even added my own strong feelings that a child can learn some pretty positive things from a hospital experience and an operation, if it is handled right. A great deal of learning about oneself in childhood comes about under stressful situations. And if a child learns that she can cope with pain, with being in a strange, frightening place away from home, can learn how to manage for herself at times, can see that people like doctors and nurses want to help even though they hurt her, and can then see that the operation has made her feel better—all of these can add up to a positive experience in learning how to master the world. I am convinced that even small children

---

*President: Mrs. Judy Grove, 176 N. Villa, Villa Park, Illinois, 60181.
†#1 Wilshire Park, Needham, Massachusetts, 12192.

can and do gather confidence in themselves and those around them through such an experience.

Not only have we found that we can prevent traumatic reactions to the separation and pain of hospitalization by properly preparing small children, but we have been impressed with the fact that many children can use a hospital experience as a positive one. If they come through it safely and, with moral support, can deal with it, a child can feel she has achieved something *herself.* In other words, the experience can be seen by the child as a sign of coping successfully. This is worth helping her to achieve.

PREPARING THE CHILD

It is important that adults help a child as much as they can, and Mrs. Landis was aware of this. I could answer her first question without any qualms. She certainly should and must prepare Tommy for as much of it as she could. She should tell him what to expect in as much detail as she knew herself. There are booklets which are availble from most pediatric hospitals which give details about the procedures which can be expected. These booklets are descriptive and help the mother and child be prepared for the steps which will be taken on any admission. It is then important for a parent to go into further detail to describe what the child will be likely to encounter in her own circumstances. If a parent isn't aware of what these things will be, she should call the surgeon's office or the hospital for details of what they can expect. Preparation *by the parent* for each of these steps becomes a terribly important and reassuring backup for the child.

I wished that pre-admission visits could be arranged in all hospitals for the children who were going to be admitted. We have done this at Children's Hospital in Boston and it works wonderfully. Actually seeing a frightening situation ahead of time, particularly in the company of one's parents, can be reassuring. We know that children who must go through cardiac surgery do much better in the critical postoperative period if they have been shown an oxygen tent and allowed to get into it, if they have been taken into the recovery room and the room where they will receive treatments, *and* if they are introduced to a child who has been through it all and is recovering. This last step is of great importance, for children are like adults. They can overcome a great deal of anxiety and pain if they know someone else with whom they can identify has done it. Children who will not be as sick as these postoperative cardiac patients also can profit by knowing what will happen and that others have gone through it all. I remember one terrified little black boy who sat bolt upright, rocking in his crib after an operation, sucking his thumb and clinging to a piece of his mother's clothing which she'd left with him. As he rocked, and whimpered in pain, he kept humming a tune and whispering words to it. When I leaned down to listen to his words, he was singing over and over to himself, "My momma told me this would happen." Indeed, she had told him some of the things he could expect, but not all of them. But the fact that she'd been willing to prepare him for a few of them served to shore him up when she wasn't there. He clung to her remembered words and to her scarf as if she were there. Her preparation was critical to him as he adjusted to the hospitalization and to the postoperative trauma. After he went home, he refused to let her out of his sight. Otherwise, he made a remarkable recovery. Later, he remembered that she'd been there with him "most of the time."

Our Boston Children's Museum has a popular exhibit to prepare the hundreds of children who might go to the hospital without any warning. The exhibit consists of very little beside a hospital bed, a series of white coats, and a few stethoscopes, giving children the opportunity to play at being sick in the hospital room. It is always crowded, and at any one time you can hear a child proudly telling his awestruck companions about his experience in a hospital. I am sure that even as superficial an exposure as this exhibit becomes a tremendously reassuring memory for a frightened child when he must be admitted in pain to a hospital bed.

Mrs. Landis winced as I suggested that she warn Tom about the necessary needles and injections, and about having to leave him at the time of operation, as well as the sore throat he would have after it was over. "But wouldn't it just scare him to tell him in advance? Wouldn't it be easier for me to comfort him after it was over and to help him *then*?" I agreed with her that telling him too far (more than a day or so) in advance was unnecessary. But if she could handle her own anxiety about these necessary events, the memory of her explanation would reassure him when they happened. The unknown and unexpected is far more frightening for children than is fear of pain for which they are prepared, even though they may protest more vigorously at the time. In addition to the anxiety which is dispelled by preparation for each step in such an experience, the child's trust in her parents and their ability to protect her are tremendously reinforced if the child has seen that they themselves are not overwhelmed by this strange, new experience.

When we sampled a group of parents who were bringing their small children in to the Boston Children's Hospital Medical Center for planned admissions and who had been urged to prepare these children with a booklet explaining the hospital and its procedures, we found that only 15% of these parents had read the booklet to their children before they came in. We tried to find out why these presumably well-intentioned parents had ignored our advice to prepare their children. In each case, they shyly admitted that they themselves couldn't face the impending separation and trauma, and couldn't bear discussing it with the child. Since we knew it was important to the child that his own parent discuss it with him, we arranged to have one of our team be with each of these parents while they read the booklet to the child—often with tears in their eyes. The value of this to the child after she was on the ward of the hospital was so obvious to us that we have continued to press parents to prepare each child. With such preparation from their own parents, children do not become as frightened or as withdrawn, and they eat, sleep, and recover better both in the hospital and after they return home.

I urged Mrs. Landis to find out as many details about the things Tommy would have to do, where he would stay, what kind of medication and anesthesia he would have, how long he would be there, and she agreed to tell him the truth about as many of these details as she could—on the day before he was to be admitted. If he asked questions, which we hoped he would, she was to answer them as truthfully and in as much detail as she could. I urged her to call me if she floundered or felt like wavering, so that I could remind her how important all this was to Tommy.

"What other preparations could I make that would make a difference to him?" Tommy had a beloved teddy bear which was torn and frayed and exuded its stuffing. I urged her to wash and to sew up the edges of his teddy so it would not lose its contents all over the hospital bed. I wanted it to be respected by the hospital personnel as an important companion for Tommy in distress. A child's own precious things, his own clothes, and even a picture of his family are of great comfort at such a time.

STAYING AT THE HOSPITAL

In answer to her question about whether she should be with him in the hospital, I was as definite as I could be. "Of course you should. This is a time when a child needs security and comfort more than any other. Why should he not have it from you and his father?" She replied that the hospital where Tommy was going to be didn't want parents around. They had stated that the nurses and doctors know the most about caring for a sick child and that parents often interfered by being too fluttery and anxious, passing their own anxiety on to the child. Hospital personnel also had found that children cried more when parents were with them, and were quieter and rested more without them. Since it was a short two-day stay, the hospital personnel were convinced it was better for the child to be left alone to recover and to be gathered up the day after the operation. When I asked Mrs. Landis what she thought about all of this, she said, "Well, I don't really believe it. But it *is* my fault that Tommy has been sick so much, and he may really do better with the more competent medical staff. I certainly wouldn't know how to care for him. I'm sure he would cry more if I were there. So I was ready to buy their explanations—until I talked to you. Now you make me feel guilty for being afraid to fight to stay with Tommy."

In this rather sad acceptance of the hospital's dicta, I could see all the guilty helplessness that mothers feel guilty about any illness in their child. I now expect caring mothers to feel guilty about anything that happens to their children, whether they can indeed be considered culpable or not. Inherent in caring about a child is the feeling that anything that goes wrong is the responsibility of the adult. Quite often, as in Mrs. Landis' case, this feeling of responsibility and inadequacy is not founded on fact. It also interferes with doing necessary things for her. This feeling of helplessness is understandable in the face of an overpowering, expert hospital staff, which plays on natural feelings of guilt and inadequacy. Fathers feel the same way. Parents may over-react to these feelings and become combative or belligerent with hospital staff who do not even attempt to understand them. Parents in this situation indeed do become problems on the ward and can interfere with the child's optimal care. In hospitals where the staff is trained to understand these as natural, healthy feelings in bereft parents, and where there is provision for incorporating the parents into the care of the sick child, these same "helpless" parents can be a major asset. In the Parent Participation Unit of Riley Children's Hospital in Indianapolis, not only have the costs of hospital care been cut in half, but children improve more quickly, and parents *learn* to care for their sick child while she (and they) are under the safe supervision of a knowledgeable hospital staff. Of course parents are frightened and feel inadequate and helpless for a sick child, but they can and do learn how to cope with very little help. The value to the ill child is obvious—not only of having her parents nearby, but of having them in the old familiar role of taking care of her. She may be able to see herself in this old healthy image rather than in the new sick one. She certainly will be likely to handle her illness better.

I do *not* feel that children do better with strangers, no matter how competent. I do not feel that parents will pass on their own anxiety to the child unless they are given no other outlet. The hospital staff should be able to recognize this anxiety and help parents with it. I am sure that it is not harmful for children to cry who are miserable or in pain. In fact I happen to think it's good for them at such a time. It stirs up their vascular and respiratory systems to a vigorous response which may even speed recovery. It also gives them a feeling of being able to do something about their misery, of being able to protest with hope for comfort. When they do receive comfort and do begin to recover, they may even feel it is partly *because* they protested. Protest is a healthy mechanism! John Bowlby, an eminent child analyst in England, pointed out that there were three stages of response which children showed when they were ill and hospitalized: (1) protest; (2) despair, often seen in children who are "too good" and accept everything that is done to them too readily; and (3) detachment and severe depression—seen in children who literally turn to the wall, away from the dangerous, unrewarding environment around them. These three stages of response to an overwhelming situation represent an increasing degree of seriousness. From them one can predict the kind of recovery the child will make. After the physical illness is over, the children who have regressed to Stage 3 may be left with serious psychopathology such as severe bedwetting, fears, depression, etc. Those in Stage 2 may have suffered a serious rift in their feelings of trust toward the environment around them. They are likely to blame themselves for everything that happens as if it were a just punishment for their badness. One 4-year-old with rheumatic fever told me that she would never have gotten sick and been sent to the hospital if she'd stayed a good girl all the time. This kind of self-punishment in childhood can lead to adults who are crippled emotionally. As long as a child is protesting, is fighting for her rights, is crying when it is safe to do so, I am convinced that she's putting up the healthiest battle she can. I'm also sure she'll come out of such an event without too much psychological scarring.

I certainly wouldn't agree with Mrs. Landis' report from the hospital that two days is too short to worry about. For a child, any separation, particularly under such frightening and painful conditions, is too long to ignore. I urged Mrs. Landis to demand that she be allowed to stay with Tommy. Most hospitals are aware of the need to change such outdated practices as that of keeping parents away and will adjust if a parent stands firm. She can press for being allowed to stay, without requiring a bed or rooming-in arrangement. She can even prop herself up in a chair for the night and let her husband spell her. As Tommy becomes accustomed to his new surroundings, he might not even need one of them the next night. But I wanted *her* to demand the option and not to leave it up to the biased hospital personnel. I warned her that the attitude she had encountered at the hospital meant that they would continue to be unaccepting of her, and that she mustn't expect them to want her to do things for Tommy. Even if she were stripped of her dignity and of her role as a mother for the two days, her very presence as an anchoring reassurance was of vital importance to him. If she could prove to the staff that her presence was comforting to him and that she needn't get in the way of their doing a good job by him, perhaps she might affect their future policy for other parents. It is certainly time for all hospitals to reconsider their policy in respect to parents being present. I feel that we now know enough about children's reactions to separation and hospitalization to make it universally possible for parents to be with their children through such procedures rather than leaving it to chance or expediency. Certainly there are many situations where this isn't possible for the parents— for instance, in the case of a mother with other small children for whom she has no sitter. And in cases where the child must be hospitalized for a long period, a parent's constant presence could drain the rest of the family—both financially and psychologically. In these cases, there are other ways of helping children through crises. There can be substitute mothers on the ward, grandparents or their substitutes*, play ladies who make a special effort to involve the child in therapeutic play around the issues of illness and separation. The emphasis of the entire team concerned with the child's recovery must be on her psychological as well as on her physical recovery.

If a mother can't be present all the time, she must prepare the child for her leaving. She should also give the child a time when she will return and try to abide by it. If she can, she might leave the child with a special "lovey" or resource of her own. She might try to call someone over who will stay to help the child with the acute separation. When she returns, it will reinforce the child's trust for future

---

*There is a program for "Substitute Grandparents" on children's wards, funded by the Office of Child Development, from which both generations profit.

separations, if she reminds her that she promised to return: "Here I am."

Mothers too often feel so bereft themselves that they tend to desert the child without warning. This is not fair to the child. Letting her learn to cope alone may be a positive learning experience—but only if it is couched in a trusting relationship. Lying to a child or running away from her at such a time will certainly not promote trust for the future.

AGE DIFFERENCES

The age of the child who must be hospitalized may influence the kind of concerns which she has. In children who are smalller than 5 or 6 years, separation from home and parents is a more terrifying aspect of the experience than the pain or illness she must endure. Separation magnifies fear and, by the same token, having a parent to rely on decreases it. From 4 years on, fears of being damaged or hurt begin to be of more and more importance, and the importance of having a parent nearby may be that the child feels she has some control over the danger of being mutilated. As the child gets to preadolescence, a parent's presence may not be nearly as important as the staff's being aware of her need to master anxiety about damage to herself. For older children, programs which aim at reinforcing their self-images and their sense of being in control are of vital importance. At Tommy's age, concerns about separation and about mutilation are both liable to be operating. In order to help him with his fears about being damaged or about losing a part of himself—and with an operation aimed at removing such a part, however useless—his parents must remember that his concerns about being intact are uppermost. They must bring this out in the open and talk about it, in order to help him understand the difference between fears and the reality of having lost an unnecessary part of himself.

REACTIONS TO HOSPITALIZATION

Mrs. Landis' last questions were harder to answer until he came home. Each child has an unpredictably different response to such an experience. He might be angry with her when he came home, and he might reward her efforts to comfort and reassure him with resentful behavior. She showed me her concern about his turning on her, and I was afraid that she'd be pretty upset when he did. So I tried to help her understand that he had no other way of working out his anxiety or his pent-up anger. Children rarely blow up in the hospital, although they may fight and protest valiantly. But it isn't until they return home and are safe that they dare to begin to show their real feelings and they nearly always take them out on the safest people around—their parents. This is healthy and it may help Mrs. Landis to know that it is. She still may feel hurt, for it is hard to take a child's temper tantrums as a reward for having struggled to help him through such an ordeal.

Many of the reactions that Tommy will show can be summed up as "regression." He may begin to act like a baby—he may cry a lot more, cling to either or both parents; he may become more violent and unrestrained in beating on his younger brother; he may begin to wet his bed again, or to suck his thumb; he may want to be carried or rocked as he did when he was much younger. This regressive behavior can be seen as normal and to serving a real purpose. By returning to an earlier level of adjustment, Tommy can conserve his energy and gather more attention from those around him. Mrs. Landis will need to see this behavior for what it is. She should try to put up with it for a while, help Tommy understand why he needs to regress in his behavior, and then encourage and support him to want to grow up again, after he's had a chance to work through his experience. Punishment might well get rid of the more childish behavior, but not in a healthy way. It would shove his feelings underground, where they will not serve any but a destructive purpose. He needs positive support and encouragement to recover his threatened image of himself. In a study of normal children, over 50% used regressive behavior over a six-month recovery period after a hospitalization, however brief the hospitalization was. It is normal and healthy for children to step back while they gather energy to move forward again.

I urged Mrs. Landis to continue to talk to Tommy about his experiences after he came home, to urge him to play them out, and to talk them out if he could. Primarily, I felt it important that she and his father be aware that no matter how well they prepared and supported him the operation might still be a scary experience. But if *he* could see it as one that he had gotten through himself, had conquered, with his parents there to rely on, *then* the operation could become a real learning experience. Children thus fortified are on their way to coping with their own world, no matter what it deals them.

GUIDELINES

1. Prepare a child by describing the hospitalization in as much detail as you can beforehand. If you don't know all of the events which will affect her, a few, described in detail, will help a lot. The nurses in charge of the floor she will go to, or the doctor's assistant should be able to tell you some of the procedures she will experience. It's worth preparing yourself as well.

2. Plan to stay with your child in the hospital if at all possible. If you have to leave for periods, be sure to tell her why and when you will return. Be back when you said you would.

3. Remember that crying in protest to your leaving or to a painful procedure is a healthy expression of her feelings. Don't try to make her stop or to feel guilty about them. If she cries for a long time, point that out to her, but say it's not bad, just hard on everyone else around her.

4. If you can, accompany her to the operating room and to the treatment room for any painful procedure. If you can't go in with her to hold her hand, let her know that in advance. Remind her that you will be waiting for her afterward. Explain that you can't control everything for her here like you do at home—and tell her why. Reiterating to her that the painful procedures will not do her permanent damage, but that they do hurt and frighten, gives her permission to "let off steam" and to expose her fears of being mutilated—these are universal. Explain that these very procedures will make her better eventually. She needn't be expected to believe you, of course, but she may remember it and be reminded of it later. Having trust in authorities is a very precious result of an hospital experience.

5. Once at home, continue to talk about the hospital experience, as long as the child seems threatened. Reassure her that her regression is part of having been ill and is not a sign that she's "bad" or a "baby." Listen to her and help her to understand herself.

ABOUT THE AUTHOR

T. Berry Brazelton, M.D., is Clinical Professor of Pediatrics Emeritus at Harvard Medical School and founder of the Child Development Unit at the Boston Children's Hospital Medical Center. The Brazelton Neonatal Behavioral Assessment Scale is in use in major hospitals throughout the United States and abroad. The American Academy of Pediatrics awarded Dr. Brazelton the prestigious C. Anderson Aldrich Award for Outstanding Contributions to the Field of Child Development. Aside from his numerous scholarly publications, he is well known to parents as the author of many books, including *Infants and Mothers, Toddlers and Parents, On Becoming a Family,* and *Working and Caring.* Dr. Brazelton is equally familiar to television viewers as the host of his series "What Every Baby Knows" on Lifetime Cable Television Network.

INDEX

Abdominal pain. *See* Stomachaches
Adenoids, removal of, 167–168
Adolescence, developmental signs
    of, 6
Adrenalin, 146, 154
Aggression, and fears, 36–39, 41–42
Alcohol rub, 141
Allergens, 148–149, 150–151, 153–154
Allergies. *See* Asthma
Als, Heidelise, 22, 34
Altruism, as parental goal, 86–87
Aminophyllin, 153, 154
Anders, Thomas F., 100
Anorexia, 6
Antibiotics, 151–152
Antihistamines, 150, 151
Antispasmodics, 151
Anxiety, and illness, 8, 10, 125–126,
    134
Appendicitis, 2, 129
Appetite, lack of, 6
    See also Feeding
Aspirin, 132, 134, 142
Asthma, 145–155
    allergens and, 148–149,
      150–151, 153–154
    avoiding fear and panic,
      146–147

colds and, 149–152
    guidelines for dealing with,
      153–155
    importance of prevention,
      147–149
    including child in prevention
      and treatment of, 152–153
    medication for, 146, 153, 154
    parents' reaction to, 8–9
    wheezing in, 138, 146, 151,
      152–153, 154
Autonomy. *See* Independence

Babies. *See* Infants
Barr, Ron, 130
Bedwetting, 157–165
    guidelines for dealing with,
      164–165
    following hospitalization, 176
    new siblings and, 77
    parents' reaction to, 2
    psychological problems of,
      157–160
    as transitory behavior, 1, 5, 6
Bellyaches. *See* Stomachaches
Bladder control. *See* Bedwetting;
    Toilet training

Blood sugar:
    headaches and, 131, 133–134
    midmorning drop in, 133
    stomachaches and, 130
Body image, in adolescence, 6
Bowel movements, of infants, 5
    See also Constipation; Toilet
        training
Bowlby, John, 168, 173
Boys:
    bedwetting by (*see* Bedwetting)
    developmental signs in, 5
    headaches of, 5 (*see also* Head-
        aches)
    stomachaches of, 129–130
Breastfeeding:
    allergies and, 148–149, 154
    bowel movements and, 5
    decision on, 95
    external stimuli and, 99
    fathers and, 95–97
    in large families, 76
    milk in, 95, 148
    spacing of children and, 71
    success in, 76, 95
    sucking and, 61
    weaning and, 70, 94
Breath-holding spells, 5
Breathing difficulties:
    in convulsions, 141
    with croup, 138–139
    tensions and, 8
    See also Asthma
Bronchitis, 138
Burping, 97

Child Health Encyclopedia (Fein-
    bloom), 143
Children in Hospitals, 168
Chocolate, as allergen, 149
Colds, 149–152
Colic:
    in hypersensitive infants, 28
    as transitory symptom, 5
Committee on Psychosocial Develop-
    ment of Children and Fami-
    lies, 12
Communication:
    between father and infant,
        24–25
    between mother and infant,
        23–24
    sadness and, 52

Competence, sense of, 56
Constipation:
    in early school years, 6
    in infants, 5
    stomachaches and, 126, 127
Convulsions, 140–142
Croup, 137–140
Crying:
    of hypersensitive infants, 28
    sadness vs., 45

Demanding behavior. *See* Tantrums
Depression. *See* Sadness
Diarrhea:
    as allergic reaction, 154
    in hypersensitive infants, 28
Discipline, 81–90
    behavior disturbances and,
        16–17
    guidelines for, 87–90
    need for, 81–85
    parental goals and, 86–87
    physical punishment, 88
    socialization and, 86–87
    strictness and, 89–90
    See also Limit-setting
Dixon, Suzanne, 24, 34
Doctor and Child (Brazelton), 45,
    162
Doctors. *See* Physicians
Dogs, fear of, 40
    See also Pets
Dolls. *See* Loveys
Dreams, 40

Ear infections, 167
Eczema, 145, 147, 148, 149, 150
Eggs, as allergens, 149
Emde, Robert N., 108
Emergencies, 137–143
    convulsions, 140–142
    croup, 137–140
    poisoning, 142–143
Emetics, 143
Enemas, 127
Enuresis. *See* Bedwetting
Erikson, Erik, 36
"Essen und brechen" philosophy, 98,
    101
Examination, physical:
    anxiety about, 38
    use of teddy bear in, 64–65

Family Bed, The (Thevenin), 112
Fathers:
    communication with infants,
      24–25
    feeding by, 95–97
    play and, 24–25
Fears, 33–42
    aggression and, 36–39, 41–42
    as developmental sign, 5
    of dogs, 40
    dreams and, 40
    facing, 40–41
    guidelines for dealing with,
      41–42
    limit-setting and, 40, 41
    of loud noises, 35–36
    of physical examinations, 38
    in second year, 35–36
    stranger anxiety, 33–35
    tantrums and, 36
Feathers, as allergens, 150, 154
Feedback system:
    between father and infant,
      24–25
    hypersensitive infants and,
      26–30
    love and, 25–26
    between mother and infant,
      23–24
Feeding, 93–105
    burping and, 97
    difficulties in, 97, 98–99, 100,
      101–103
    by fathers, 95–97
    guidelines for, 104–105
    independence and, 100–103
    of infants, 95–101
    negativism and, 102, 103
    nutrition and, 93–95, 104
    patterns in, 98–99
    of toddlers, 101–103
    See also Breastfeeding
Feinbloom, Richard I., 143
Fever, with convulsions, 140, 141–142
Fingersucking:
    as developmental sign, 5
    need for, 58–59, 60–63
    parents' concerns about, 58–60
    See also Thumbsucking
Fish, as allergen, 149
Food:
    allergenic, 148–149, 153–154
    minimum daily requirements
      for, 104

    playing with, 102, 103
    refusal of, 5, 98, 99, 101, 102
Fraiberg, Selma, 36
Fruit, 104

Grief, 46–49

Headaches, 131–132
    blood sugar and, 131, 133
    in boys, 5
    guidelines for, 135
    medications for, 132, 134
    migraine, 131, 134, 135
    school fears and, 6–7
    severe, 131–132, 134
    stress and, 132–134
Hives, 149
Horsehair, as allergen, 150, 154
Hospitalization, 167–177
    age and, 175
    guidelines for dealing with, 177
    making a positive experience,
      168–169
    need for loveys during, 171, 174
    parents staying with child,
      171–175, 177
    preparing the child, 169–171
    reactions to, 175–176
    regression following, 176
    self-blame for, 173
Hypersensitive infants, 26–30, 58
Hypoglycemia, 133

Illness:
    anxiety and, 8, 10, 125–126
    faking of, 9
    physicians and, 10–11
    See also Psychosomatic
      disorders
Inadequacy feelings, 49–51
Independence:
    feeding and, 100–103
    of infants, 26, 55–56, 70–71,
      72–73, 100–101
    at night, 111, 112, 114–117
    pressures for, 55–56
    sleep problems and, 114–117
    spacing of children and, 70–71,
      72–73
    of toddlers, 72–73, 111, 112,
      114–117, 119–120

Infants:
    causes of night waking in,
        110–112
    closely spaced, 71–72
    developmental signs of, 5
    failure to thrive, 22–23
    fathers and, 24–25
    feeding of, 95–101
    frowning by, 27
    hypersensitive, 26–30
    independence of 26, 55–56,
        70–71, 72–73, 100–101
    learning about love, 21–30
    limit-setting for, 26, 30
    mothers and, 23–24
    need for loveys, 56–59
    need for sucking, 57–58, 59,
        60–63
    nurturing by siblings, 74–75
    sleep cycles of, 108–110
    sleeping in parents' bed, 112,
        113, 118–120
    stranger anxiety and, 33–35
    varied reactions of, 2–3
Ipecac, 143
Irish twins, 71

Kaye, Kenneth, 98
Kwashiorkor, 94, 113

Leg aches, 131
Limit-setting:
    behavior disturbances and,
        16–17
    fears and, 40, 41
    for infants, 26, 30
    as love, 30
    need for, 82–85
    as parental goal, 86
    See also Discipline
Loss, and sadness, 46–49
Love, 21–30
    between father and infant, 24–25
    feedback system and, 25–26
    hypersensitive infants and, 26–30
    between mother and infant,
        23–24
Loveys:
    care of, 65
    hospitalized children and, 171,
        174
    need for, 56, 59, 64–65

pacifiers and, 63
parental conerns about, 58–60
sleep and, 116–117, 118, 121,
    122
Lying, 1, 5

MacKeith, Ronald, 160
Magic Years, The (Fraiberg), 36
Marital discord, 9–10
Mastery, awareness of, 56
Masturbation:
    as developmental sign, 5
    parents' reaction to, 2
Mead, Margaret, 74
Meals. *See* Feeding; Food
Medication:
    for asthma, 146, 153, 154
    for colds, 150, 151
    for croup, 140
    for headaches, 132, 134
    for infections, 151–152
    for poisoning, 143
    for seizures, 142
Menstruation, delayed onset of, 6
Migraine headaches, 131, 134, 135
Milk:
    allergies to, 148, 153–154
    breast, 95, 148
    minimum daily requirement of,
        104
    stomachaches and, 130
Minimum daily requirements, 104
Moro reflex, 57
Mothers:
    communication with infants,
        23–24
    feeding and, 93–95, 98, 101
    nutrition and, 93–95
    See also Breastfeeding

Nausea, 5
Negativism:
    feeding and, 102, 103
    need for limits and, 82, 84, 85
    new siblings and, 77
Nelsen, Christine, 143
Neocalglucon, 104
Night light, 120
Nightmares, 5
    See also Dreams
Night waking, 110–112
Noises, fear of, 35–36

Nurturing, of new babies by siblings, 74–75, 77
See also Love
Nutrition, 93–95, 104

Object permanence, 34–35
Obstipation, 131
Oedipal feelings, 40
Overeating, in adolescence, 6
Overreactive infants. *See* Hypersensitive infants

Pacifiers:
    for hypersensitive infants, 29
    loveys and, 63
    need for, 56
    as substitutes for fingersucking, 63
Parents Concerned for Hospitalized Children, 168
Parmelee, Arthur H., Jr., 108
Peers:
    self-image and, 51
    toddlers and, 73
Permissiveness, 81–85
    See also Discipline; Limit-setting
Pets:
    as allergens, 151
    grief over loss of, 46, 47
Phenobarbital, 142
Physicians, 10–11, 38
Piaget, Jean, 56
Play:
    fathers and, 24–25
    as outlet for negativism, 77
Poisioning, 142–143
Potty chair, 160 161
Pregnancy (ies):
    nutrition and, 93–94
    sleep cycles and, 109
    spacing of, 69–77
Prodrome, 131
Protein requirements, 104
Psychosomatic disorders, 125–126
    asthma, 8–9, 145–155
    bedwetting, 1, 2, 5, 77, 157–165
    convulsions, 140–142
    croup, 137–140
    headaches, 5, 6–7, 131–132, 135
    hospitalization, 167–177
    multiple triggers of, 132–134
    parental anxiety and, 8–9
    physicians and, 10

poisoning, 142–143
stomachaches, 1, 2, 6, 126–131, 135
stress and, 132–134
Punishment. *See* Discipline

Rash, as allergic reaction, 154
Regurgitation. *See* Spitting up; Vomiting
Reingold, Harriet, 35
REM sleep, 110, 111
Respiratory infections, 149–152, 154
Reyes' syndrome, 142n
Rumination, 4

Sadness, 45–53
    crying vs., 45
    feelings of inadequacy and, 49–51
    guidelines for dealing with, 52–53
    looking behind, 49–51
    loss and, 46–49
    need for attention and, 48
    recognizing, 45–46
    suicide and, 49–50
School fears:
    dealing with, 7–8
    as developmental sign, 5, 6
    headaches and, 6–7
Security blanket:
    need for, 56
    parents' concerns about, 58, 59
    washing, 65, 66
    See also Loveys
Seizures, 140–142
Self image:
    inadequacy feelings and, 49–51
    peers and, 51
Sharing, 75–76
Should I Call the Doctor? (Nelsen), 143
Sibling rivalry, 73
Siblings, 69–77
    bedwetting and, 77
    closely spaced, 71–72
    Irish twins, 71
    learning to share and, 75–76
    loss of attention and, 47, 75
    negativism and, 77
    nurturing of new babies by, 74–75, 77
    protected time with parents, 75–76

Siblings *cont'd*
    spacing of, 69–77
Sick stomach, 5
Sleep, 107–122
    cultural expectations and,
        112–114
    in family bed, 111, 112, 113,
        118–120
    feeding and, 121
    guidelines for, 120–122
    of infants, 107–112
    loveys and, 116–117, 118, 121,
        122
    of toddlers, 111–112
Sleep cycles, 108–110
Sleep problems:
    autonomy and, 114–117
    causes of night waking, 110–112
    discipline and, 13, 14, 17
Snacks, 102, 104, 133
Snoring, 150
Society for Research in Child Develop-
    ment, 12
Sounds, fear of, 35–36
Spacing of children, 69–77
    See also Siblings
Spitting up:
    as developmental sign, 5
    proper feeding and, 97
    reasons for, 3–5
    See also Vomiting
Spock, Benjamin, 81
Spoiled child, 82–85
Sports, and aggression, 42
Stealing, 1, 5
Stomachaches, 126–131
    anxiety about, 2
    appendicitis and, 2, 129
    blood sugar and, 130
    in early school years, 6
    in girls, 129–130
    guidelines for, 135
    milk and, 130
    as transitory symptom, 1, 5
    urinary infection and, 129
Stranger anxiety, 33–35
Stress, and psychosomatic disorders,
    132–134
Strictness, 89–90
Stuffed toys, as allergens, 150, 151, 154
Sucking:
    need for, 57–58, 60–63
    parents' concerns about, 58–60
    See also Thumbsucking

Suicide, 49–50
Suppositories, 127
Swaddling, 29

Tantrums:
    fears and, 36
    new siblings and, 72–73, 77
    permissiveness and, 81, 82–85
    in toddlers, 5, 87–88, 89
    as transitory stage, 5
Teasing, 87–88, 89, 103, 113
Teddy bears:
    physical examinations and,
        64–65
    repair of, 65
    See also Loveys
Thevenin, Tine, 112
Thumbsucking:
    following hospitalization, 176
    by hypersensitive infants, 29, 58
    need for, 57–58, 59, 60–63
    parents' reaction to, 3, 58–60
    as transitory behavior, 2, 5
Tics, 5
Toilet training, 5, 160–163
Tomatoes, as allergens, 149
Toys, stuffed, 150, 151, 154
    See also Loveys
Tronick, Edward, 22, 34

Undernutrition, 93–94
Urinary infection, 129

Vegetables, 101, 104
Vitamins, 104
Vomiting, as allergic reaction, 154
    See also Spitting up

Weaning, 70, 72, 94
Wheat allergies, 149
Wheezing:
    in asthma, 138, 146, 151,
        152–153, 154
    in bronchitis, 138
    in croup, 138–139
White, Robert, 56

Yogman, Michael, 24, 34